LAUGH YOUR WAY TO
REAL
ESTATE
SALES SUCCESS

For Real Estate Agents, WannaBes, UsedToBes, & Those Who Love Them!

CATHY TURNEY

LAUGH YOUR WAY TO REAL ESTATE SALES SUCCESS

For Real Estate Agents, WannaBes, UsedToBes, and Those Who Love Them!

For Marion,
who raised a wonderful
family in a beautiful
home. *XOXO, Cathy*

CATHY TURNEY

Laugh Your Way to Real Estate Sales Success

For Real Estate Agents, WannaBes, UsedToBes, and Those Who Love Them!

Cathy Turney

Published by: Real Estate Success Press

www.RealEstateSuccessPress.com

ISBN: 978-0692346389

Library of Congress Control Number: 2014950807

To my mother,
who started it all,
and
MyHusbandTheEngineer,
who keeps it all going.

Praise for *Laugh Your Way to Real Estate Sales Success*

"This is it—the key to unlimited success in business and in life. A twenty-five year veteran of real estate sales, Cathy Turney imparts golden lessons on getting to the top and staying there. Experienced agents will learn a few tricks; WannaBes will get insights to help them decide if real estate is the right career for them; and UsedToBes may just reconsider."

> *—John Robinson, founder of PassionQuest Technologies LLC, #1 best-selling author and master business coach*

"Thankfully, *Laugh Your Way to Real Estate Sales Success* is not another 'How to Get Rich in Real Estate' book full of unrealistic promises. It's a genuinely funny account of how one top-producing broker evolved a winning strategy. A must-read for anyone considering a career in real estate."

> *—Cathryn Michon, writer/director,* Muffin Top: A Love Story

"Cathy Turney's new book, *Laugh Your Way to Real Estate Sales Success*, is both a lot of sound advice and a lot of laughs."

> *—Chuck Lamb, past president of California Association of Realtors, former CEO of Contra Costa Association of Realtors*

"If you think real estate is unreal, read *Laugh Your Way to Real Estate Sales Success*. Cathy Turney will make you laugh, of course, but she'll also make you smart about home buying, renting, selling, and just about anything else you can do with a home, which is, after all, where the heart is."

> —*Jerry Zezima, nationally syndicated columnist for* The Stamford Advocate *and author of* Leave It to Boomer *and* The Empty Nest Chronicles

"Cathy walks her own talk. She started at the bottom in real estate and quickly became and stayed successful."

> —*Michael Gadams, past president, Contra Costa Association of Realtors and broker/ owner of Bay Area Home Sales and Evaluations*

"Cathy's real estate book is educational, very readable, and very, VERY funny. That's my appraisal!"

> —*Dave Astor, author of* Comic (and Column) Confessional, *board member of National Society of Newspaper Columnists, and recent New Jersey home seller*

"If you, the reader, do not have the privilege of knowing Cathy Turney personally, then this 'resource book' will endear her to you. Cathy's latest triumph is a delightful yet deeply thought-provoking reflection on her many dedicated years as a Realtor and real estate broker. Integrity, thoroughness, communication skills, and ingenuity constantly shine as hallmarks of her professional career."

—George Naeger, broker associate,
Prudential California Realty

"Hilarious! Witty! Spiced with wisdom! *Please don't make a move till you open this book.* Then, if you like to laugh, I don't think you'll want to put it down. Cathy Turney has given America a real page Turney! Oops, page turner!"

—Patricia Evans, internationally acclaimed
author and relationship consultant

"Cathy's attention to detail and concern for the protection of her clients are the highest in the industry. Her can-do attitude and problem-solving skills inspired me to jump from the back office to become a Realtor. Her cheerleading is empowering."

—Tanisha Avila, Realtor, Keller Williams
East Bay

"It is a pleasure to work with Cathy Turney. She exemplifies the highest standards in our industry, she gets the job done, and her clients love her."

—Bob Schwab, CMC, manager, RPM
Mortgage, Orinda, California

"This book raises the bar for others of its kind. Top-notch success tips, practical solutions to challenges, and how to consistently make money in a field that tests one's perseverance. All delivered with wit and humor."

—*Judd McIlvain, Emmy Award-winning TV and radio consumer reporter*

Table of Contents

---

1   As we all know, the term "Realtor" is a trademarked professional designation of the
     National Association of Realtors, which should be all capital letters. This is the only law
     I've ever knowingly broken. Except for U-turns.

Introduction

The Evolution of the Real Estate Business, Loosely Translated from Genesis 1

In the beginning God created the heavens and ~~the earth~~ real estate.

And God said, "Let there be light," and God called the light "day," and the darkness He called "night." And thus was created the first workday.

And God said, "Let the water be gathered to one place," and God called the dry ground at the edge of the sea prime coastal property.

And God said, "Let the earth teem with ~~living creatures~~ Realtors. Be fruitful and increase in number," which was the beginning of ruthless competition for the aforementioned property.

And God made two great lights to govern the day and the night, to separate the days. Which was the beginning of the seven-day work week and evening appointments.

And God saw that it was good, for business. And then He went and created the Bureau of Real Estate, the National Association of Realtors, and the Internet, and complicated history beyond belief.

Fellow Realtors, I feel your pain. I've been where you are. I'm still where you are. I will be here *forever*—or so I tell my clients. But by writing this book, I hope to show you the way to a happier "here."

It has been scientifically proven that endorphins coursing through your body elevate your mood, induce euphoria, and enable you to enjoy selling real estate. This book will help you achieve that state of being.

There is no profession whose every move is more scrutinized, legislated, and codified. We Realtors are charged with upholding tax law, the civil code, the penal code, and state and federal law. But are we given a code for coping? No! $#!+ still happens because no legal authority has deciphered the key to dealing with the challenges of real estate. Well, here it is—a veritable road map from here to there!

I have had a successful career in real estate. By which I mean that I have never seen the inside of a jail (although I have visited other Realtors there); I drive a nice car (which I only do because some buyers and sellers fixate on cars); and I have a nice house ("nice" being defined as small but paid for). I am sure you set similar goals for yourself when you started your career. And then you sold a house. Whoa! That was work! (*And marginally profitable?*)

Kidding aside, why should you buy this book? Because you, too, could consistently earn a six-figure income, hang scads of award plaques on your walls, speak before the Board of Realtors and on Web TV, be referred by attorneys and accountants and happy clients. *Just read this.* You won't even have to buy my ten-disc "How to Make a Million Dollars in Real Estate Without Really Trying" CD program! It's all here between the covers of this book.

Regardless of where you are in the journey (thriving real estate agent, Newbie, WannaBe, or UsedToBe) you'll find "teaching moments," stories that reveal:

- The key to staying employed
- How to protect your bottom (line)
- How to get and keep a stable of good contractors
- How to handle demanding people (agents, clients, ~~family~~)
- Ways to avoid time suck
- Alternatives to letting kids bankrupt their parents
- And quintessential tips on how to be a real estate sales whiz!

Every day, there's something new to learn in real estate. If you used to be a Realtor, these tips may boost your endorphin level and bring you back to the fold:

- The Ten Commandments: Etch these on the palm of your hand. (Chapter 7)
- Lawyers, friendly and otherwise: Forewarned is forearmed. (Chapter 9)
- The most challenging clients: See if you can top this! (Chapter 12)

- Your competition: No, this is not you—you bought my book, we're friends. (Chapter 13)

You will have permission to reproduce and distribute my ~~copyrighted~~ list of daily reminders:

- Focus.

- Breathe.

- It's not about me.

- It always works out.

- Just do it!

- I am serene.

These are provided in bullet format so that you can cut and paste them onto your computer, your car dashboard, and the forehead of any agent or client who annoys you.

The overarching message running rampant through all this insider information is that finding enjoyment and seeing humor in your real estate career will get you from point A to point Z a lot more easily. Introducing a little levity can get you through pretty much anything. Unless, of course, it's not appropriate. But most of the time it is, and it soothes nerves, appeases the opposition, and shows the public that you're both human and fun to work with. They'll want to hire you, to refer you, *to pay you.* This is vital information. Worth the price of this book! Because as infinitely personally rewarding as a career in real estate can be, someone has to pay the bills. So tuck this manual in your handbag or store it on an electronic gizmo. Think of it as "My Little Guide to Loving Real Estate." And thank you for reading it.

PART I – WHY BECOME A REALTOR?

WHY? WHY? WHY?

Chapter 1

And the Answer Is...

One doesn't usually aspire from an early age to become a salesperson, unless it's to take over Mom's or Dad's wildly successful practice. (Didn't Sylvia Porter say that most Americans' retirement plan is to inherit?) Your parents plan that you'll become a doctor, an accountant, a techie, or some other kind of professional that commands great respect and a big paycheck. *One that can repay your school loans.*

Over my twenty-five-plus years in the business, I've observed that real estate attracts nonconformists, free-thinkers, people who often fit like round pegs in square holes. Like my family. Mom, an artist at heart and real estate broker by necessity, spawned three Realtors with my dad, who studied theology at Loyola University in Chicago fully intending to become a Catholic priest. Mom said he missed his calling. He became a disabled World

War II veteran, and my oldest brother followed in his footsteps and became a disabled Vietnam veteran. They were the only two in our family who didn't go into real estate. They were the only two with steady paychecks.

I wouldn't exactly say that Realtors don't fit in anywhere else, but when a new agent joins the company he's always asked what he Used To Be. My YoungerBrotherTheRealtor used to be a CPA, but he had too much personality for that and, besides, he figured out really fast that there were bigger numbers to be had selling houses. My OtherBrotherTheRealtor used to be an auto mechanic, and I think he grew something in the hills to supplement fixing Volkswagen buses, but I can't prove it. I used to be a secretary because I didn't have the commitment to go on for a master's degree in social work and, anyway, as a Realtor I *am* a social worker.

What I'm saying here is, if you're *special* you can make it in real estate sales! There is truly a niche for (almost) everyone, no matter how unique your background. It's a field where creativity, altruism, and optimism will reward you handsomely for working hard.

But, Newbie and WannaBe, there is a learning curve. You must create an income stream. You will discover, if you haven't already, that the world conspires against real estate agents who prospect. There's the national

Do Not Call list that prevents us from randomly dialing for dollars; it's not cost effective to cross-reference the list with a phone directory. Mailing stuff? Bulk mail is not cheap, and the system has become so complex that it almost takes less time to hand-deliver a marketing piece than to sort, tag, and deliver it to the post office. Newspaper and magazine advertising are expensive, and just wait till you solicit on the web. I Googled "real estate agent" and got 142 million hits. But look at the bright side: if it were too easy, 232 million people[2] would be doing it!

My first manager told me I'd have to make one hundred calls to generate three leads, which might result in one listing. And then it might not sell (with me). Optimist that I am, I was glad it wasn't 200. I decided I needed to reach a large base but certainly not my friends and relatives, who knew I didn't know that much. So I picked a geographic "farm."[3] I was cautioned against this by all the heavy-hitting marketing gurus—they said it takes too long to get a return. Well, what else was I going to do while I wasn't selling houses?

I became an expert in my own neighborhood, wrote a newsletter, and hand-delivered it to 950 homes every month. People love things you write yourself.

---

2   Adult population in the U.S. as of May 2014.
3   Realtor talk for land with houses on it, occupied by owners who will list with you.

Maybe they enjoy finding the typos; I know my mother-in-law did until I dropped her from my list. My plan was complicated by another agent who was born and raised in the area, knew absolutely everyone, and had a stranglehold on the market there. I didn't know that when we moved into the neighborhood. So, it took me eleven months to get my first listing and a few more to get another. But I didn't starve. Fortunately, I had just remarried, and we were still honeymooning—and are to this day, in spite of real estate. Which brings me to the commission.

Repeat often: Real estate converts my unique gifts into cash flow.

Chapter 2

The Commission: It Is *Not* Fun Money

OK. Let's get this out of the way, because what is the first thing a client thinks when he thinks "Realtor"? It's "How much will this cost?" And since a good Realtor makes selling a home look so easy, many clients think it's too much. Do you hear me brother? *Am I whining?*[4]

It would be nice if we could fast-forward and replay a video of their escrow to remind them why they said at the end, "We don't pay you enough to do this," but this is earth and that would be heaven.

Six percent. That's what the client sees. Here's what we agents see: Net net net. Net #1—we catch the fish; Net #2—the fat cats eat most of it; Net #3—the remaining molecules that have not sifted through the net

---

4   No.

are ours. Landing the commission takes time and money. Not every client results in a closed escrow. There's competition: other agents, mortgage lenders who think they can sell real estate, lawyers who think they can sell real estate, relocation companies who appoint the Realtor and take 50 percent of the commission, and CPAs who convince clients that *their* Realtor friend is better than the neighborhood specialist.

Three percent. Remember this number, because that's all the agent typically gets. The 6 percent is divided, usually 50-50, between the seller's agent and the buyer's agent; and that presupposes that we actually netted a fish and negotiated it through shark-infested waters to safe harbor. At that point, the real estate company will take 40% of the 3 percent. Our split increases—if we last.

So after we net approximately 1.8 percent of the home's sale price, we apply the principle of "publish or perish." In the old days, real estate companies would pay for some newspaper and magazine advertising, open home guides, postage, paper, and even phones used on premises. Now they tell us everything is online, so "Do it yourself." True, a lot of marketing is done online, but clients still need to see the whites of our eyes on newsletters and postcards. They need to get our calendars, proving that we survived another year in real estate. *We need to spend our own money on this.*

And don't forget continuing education so that we can pay the state licensing board to stay legal. Or gas, or insurance, *or, or, or, or*.

Let's not complicate this exercise with actual numbers. Just remember—it takes a lot of fish. So, hopefully, we net enough after "or" to feed and shelter ourselves because wouldn't all this have been a huge waste of effort if we couldn't pay the IRS and the state Franchise Tax Board?

This is why when people look at the real estate commission as "fun money," *I want to scream.*

"If you think it's expensive to hire a professional to do the job, wait until you hire an amateur."

Red Adair

Chapter 3

There's Pro and There's Pro Bono

Speaking of the commission, if the definition of "professional" is that you get paid, then that must be why some of us aren't considered professional. Because we don't always get paid, and when we do it's only for part of what we do. Maybe we're semi-pros.

Take, for instance, the ambivalent seller:

"We'd like you to come over and talk to us about moving to Arizona so we can play more golf."

Me: "But you have eight golf courses within ten miles of you, you love this town, and you have a beautiful home. Why would you want to move?

Ambivalent Seller: "~~We probably don't, but we like to hear how much our house has appreciated.~~ Why don't you just come over, and we'll talk about it."

And so I will spend a few hours pulling the market data, myself, and my car together to educate them for two hours. This exercise is repeated annually because I am Number One on their hit list.

On the third visit I am taken totally by surprise because they actually decide to list their home. But they want to add $30,000 to the price, just in case. After months of open houses, weekly updates, magazine and newspaper advertising, we get a full-price offer (because the market finally caught up to them).

Ambivalent Seller: "Oh. We decided not to move to Arizona."

I chant to myself: *It is not all about the money.*

It is, however, about *some* money because you can't keep educating the public for free forever. So I've learned to screen callers over the phone. Like The Mom:

"I need to move," she declares.

"But that home has everything you ever wanted two years ago when you bought it," I remind her.

"I don't want the swimming pool anymore."

"OK. Well, last time I checked it would cost $8,000 to demo the pool. That's way less expensive than moving."

"And I want to live closer to my son."

"But he lives only two miles from you."

"And he never comes over," she sighs.

I suspect this has nothing to do with their proximity to each other, so we have an hour-long, deeply emotional discussion about sons, family, the high price of wheat in Russia, and resolve the issue over the phone at no expense to her and minimal expense to me. Because I must reserve some of my time for the paying customers.

Talk is cheaper than gas. But set a timer.

Chapter 4

Before I Became a Realtor I Was a Human Being

There are a lot of misconceptions about Realtors. We don't eat our young, most of us can't be bought, and I only tell white lies.

I would *so* like to explain on occasion, "Dear layperson, when we meet please don't assume that what brought us together was my desire to sell your home out from under you—even if you did call me to convince your husband that you need a more impressive house."

I try so hard to appear to be a normal person. Like at parties:

"Hi," I greeted Norma. "I'm Cathy, John's wife, a stepmother, good friend, enabler of two dogs, animal rescue volunteer."

Apparently, my other identity preceded me, and with eyes as big as saucers, she responded:

"Ohhhhhh—Alice the Agent is my best friend."

"Mine, too!" (One of those white lies I mentioned, but Alice is OK.)

Revealing that you're a Realtor can be like holding a crucifix to a vampire, a very effective repellent.

Does your dentist ask you to move the latte away from your mouth so he can peer into it when you see him at Starbucks? Does your CPA remind you that you can't afford prime rib when you meet at Safeway? Well, I don't talk shop in a social setting, particularly when accompanied by my husband because we've agreed that during that little itsy bitsy teensy tiny portion of my life I will focus on trying to be good company, which precludes discussing work. And:

"You need to take more time for yourself, sweetheart," he once remarked.

"Agreed! What would you like me to give up—microwaving, laundry, or walking the dogs?"

Speaking of significant others, many Realtors encourage theirs to take up hobbies, so that when you drag in at 10 p.m. he'll greet you with, "What? Home so soon?"

Real estate transforms you. You learn to choose words carefully, using relatively innocuous synonyms for "picky" (particular), "teardown" (not cost effective to repair), "broke" (financially challenged). You *never* utter HUD swear words and phrases, such as "low-income neighborhood," "no children allowed," or "handicapped need not apply." You remember, above all, not to put anything in writing that you wouldn't want read back to you in court.

My high school science teacher used me as an example to demonstrate how quickly blood flows to the face when one is mercilessly teased in front of a class of insecure teenagers. Not much fazes me anymore; real estate numbs me daily. Step into a client's home, trip, and fall flat on my face? Done that. Walk down the staircase with a buyer at my side and see the reflection of my open zipper fly in the mirror? Yep.

I define "friend" as one who will still speak to me after a nine-month hiatus during which I was putting out fires, counseling warring factions, eating, and sleeping. I buy belated birthday cards by the box.

I have become enthusiastic! Because if I'm not, how can I expect my clients to be? Besides, I am just so grateful to the people who put their trust in me that I can't contain myself—I sign many of my communiqués

"XO, Cathy." I eschew the traditional "sincerely" and "best wishes"—they sound so stilted and I just can't bring myself to simply type my name at the end of an e-mail which is what you're supposed to do because, after all, e-mail is not a letter and is supposed to be concise. This has led me down a rabbit hole on occasion.

"Thanks a million for agreeing to hold that open house for me, Jack. XO, Cathy"

"You must have misread my e-mail. I didn't. Jack"

"Oh. Cathy"

Who knows what he may have read into my missing "XO," but how can you be enthusiastic about someone letting you down?

I should probably back off a bit and just use "X"s. I can muster up an "X" even when disappointed. But I'm in too deep. Everyone I communicate with would wonder what they had done to not warrant an "O." And when there's a chain of e-mails involving multiple entities, you can't just "XO" one and not the others. It's a vicious circle.

To quote Dale Carnegie, "Flaming enthusiasm, backed up by horse sense and persistence, is the quality that most frequently makes for success." So I just go with it.

Occasionally (infrequently), though, my enthusiasm wanes, which is a sure sign of a caffeine emergency or impending flu bug. Despite our best efforts at cultivating superhuman qualities, we Realtors are still vulnerable to communicable diseases. And that is why I didn't appreciate it when the couple from San Francisco, whom I'd picked up at the train station, announced that they had ~~bubonic plague~~ raging colds, but that they would tough it out "house hunting" all afternoon. In my car. In the dead of winter (it was—it was forty degrees, in California).

"It's cold in this car," he sniffled.

"It's freezing," she said.

"I can't hear you—wind shear factor, you know?" I commented.

And thanks to fresh air and his inhaler prematurely running dry, I did not catch their disease.

Nor did I appreciate it when Harvey ignored my ~~plea~~ suggestion that he stay home, all warm and cozy with his stomach flu, and I'd scan and send the purchase offer to him so we could review it over the phone. Suffice it to say, it's a good thing I brought two copies.

So, we are human beings who have been transformed—into Realtors. But we didn't come by this persona naturally. Read on to see what makes us the way we are.

Make time to be normal.

PART II – INDOCTRINATION

Chapter 5

Be Nice–How To

If you're not nice in real estate, clients won't hire you, contractors won't work with you, and your spouse... oops! Too late? Many people in the course of my career have said to me, "You're too nice." I ask, "And how is that not working for me?"

Nice is not a synonym for pushover. Nice is fair, considerate, empathetic. It's feeling their pain, not being one. Throw some love in there while you're at it: love is patient; love is kind.

Working with our fellow Realtors should not be an adversarial endeavor. We're all in it to accomplish the same goal—sell houses. You can do it the hard way, or you can do it with grace and humor. Laughing through hassles (when appropriate) gets the other parties on board. The beauty of real estate is that if you happen to work with someone who refuses to play nice, the misery ends in a few months. You can spend their "thank you" gift money on a reward for yourself.

I will tolerate a lot if you pay me. That's not to say that I am mercenary. There are things I won't do for love or money—for instance, cooking. But when someone shows he values my time enough to hire me, well, as my husband says, I treat them better than family.[5] Don't we all want to be appreciated?

Many of us have had a friend who thinks that our lockbox key is her passport to hours of entertainment. Looking at houses may be fun to laypeople, but I was raised by a Realtor, my family is crawling with Realtors, and the last thing I want to do when I'm not trying to be the best broker you ever hire is look at more houses. (Especially since there aren't many Victorian homes where I work.)

You know her—Looky Lou, the friend who suffers from TMTOHH (too much time on her hands). Her hobby is to walk through the neighborhood, call you about signs she sees and suggest that we "just pop over and take a peek." A busy Realtor doesn't just pop over anywhere. Going to the bathroom requires scheduling. She has to log on to the computer, find the listing, maybe it's not there yet, call Looky Lou back and discuss the additional

---

5   Time—he's just saying I spend more time with them.

two she found while you were trying to help the paying customers. Inevitably, one of the listings will be available to show, so you call the seller, make an appointment, take Lou over there, listen for an hour to her describing all the improvements that she would make only she won't because she has no intention of paying anywhere near the price the seller is asking. In fact, she has no intention of buying an investment property at all. She's just bored.

"Well, it's good for you to get out and see the inventory," she rationalizes to you.

So I have developed some verbiage to help you with these friends:[6]

> Verbiage Number One: "You know, I'm swamped right now, and I'm just not going to have enough time to do all our due diligence if you see a house you want. If you're really thinking about buying something, let me refer you to some agents who are active in the purchase market." That will flush out her true intent, because if she's not sincere about buying she probably won't have you refer her; it's harder to take advantage of a stranger. If it comes to that, give her three names and don't take a referral fee.

---

6   Another freebie for buying my book.

<u>Verbiage Number Two</u>: "Oh, wow, I'm swamped. Let's see if they have an open house this weekend." If there's no open house, revert to Verbiage Number One.

Real estate is business. It is not a hobby. We sell our time and expertise.

I believe you should be as nice as you can to everyone who puts his best efforts forth on your behalf. Incentivize the contractor who isn't assured of getting your job by giving him $50 just for coming out (unless he already charges $100 for that). Tell him honestly that the seller is getting multiple bids, but you value his time. His heart will swell, and after a string of losing bids in a hot real estate market, he'll still call you back.

We need a stable of contractors; it's important to get multiple bids to convince the homeowner that he's not paying too much for a service. And if the seller has his own contractor (or unlicensed brother-in-law), you can convince him to use someone who won't land him in court.

After a while, though, $50 won't pencil out for a busy tradesman. So now and then, ask the client if, after all the bids are in, you can go back to that contractor and ask him to match or beat the best bid. It's not fair to do this often, but you have to be practical.

And if a worker goes above and beyond, and you know he did it just to please you (because you're so nice), send him a gift card. You've got to keep the stable full. Fifty dollars here and there results in your having a professional team to work with. Gets the job done. Makes you look good. Brings you more clients.

Be the worker's defender. When Mr. Picky complains about the divot in a roof board, remind him that he got a super deal on the price, and filler will smooth the surface out. When Mrs. Picky swishes her finger over the top of the refrigerator that The Maids just scoured and gets a smudge on her finger, exclaim, "Oh, darn, well, you won't be held to military standards and didn't they do a great job of removing the ~~black mold~~ mildew in the shower?" My fallback defense is, "Well, we could have had them do that (scrape off the preexisting paint splatters, dust the tops of the fan blades, sweep behind the cabinets in the garage), too, but it would have cost more." Use your Realtor's perspective. When desperate, I offer, "I wouldn't have done it for that price, would you?"

It's a lot of work being nice. So when it comes to my own home, I relax. I can hire someone just because I like him. I don't have to check the state Contractors Licensing Board to see if he's legal. I don't have to get multiple bids. I can let the carpet installer get away with chipping our mirrored closet door and the stucco man bring his Chihuahua for three days (my poodle loved it). I tip generously. From time to time my husband and I have a discussion about this. Usually between escrows: "You fight tooth and nail for your clients, and you let everybody walk all over us," he says.

It's hard for someone who works all day with professional engineers who bill by the hour and get bonuses to feel our pain. To understand that I just want to hire the first contractor who shows up at the door without repeated phone calls. So my answer to that is, "It's my way of thanking workers of America, the 90 percent, for being contributing members of society, for doing something that can be measured—if only by not breaking anything." It's hard to argue against charity.

"Nice" and "weak" are not synonymous.

Chapter 6

Let's Do Real Estate! Clinch Buyer and Seller Loyalty

An integral part of our Realtor culture is the office meeting, which is customarily held on Mondays. We might otherwise never know a new week had begun because Realtors don't observe weekends. These get-togethers are where you learn about what *not* to do. We learned everything that we *should* do in the real estate licensee's exam.[7]

Office meetings used to be more fun before the Insurance Commissioner concluded that everything wrong with the real estate industry could be traced back to title companies providing us with muffins.

---

7   Ha!

I wrote this nondenominational prayer to open our sessions. Kind of like what Congress does, only I acknowledge a higher authority:

> *God, grant me the serenity to accept the things I cannot change, courage to change the things I can, and wisdom to know the difference. To recognize that everything in real estate is a life or death emergency, and that I am free to work any fourteen hours of the day I wish. I will provide solace to aspiring homebuyers who can't qualify for a mortgage, marital advice to couples on the verge of divorce, temporary shelter to their pets, advice to the lovelorn, and will mediate family disputes involving inheritances. I will prescribe over-the-counter drugs to clients in need. I acknowledge that my purpose on this earth is not necessarily to have a good time, and I pledge to continually look for a job since I become unemployed after each escrow closes. Amen.*

Productive office meetings, though, require more than prayer—they need listings. Listings breed more listings and, conversely, *no* listings breeds extinction. But how do you get them? Sellers want to know that you've actually sold a house before they turn theirs over to you.

Let's Do Sellers!

We'll discuss the many qualities that make a successful listing agent, but we mustn't overlook the basics, like:

1. Money—sufficient to clean the seller's freshly steam-cleaned carpet that you spill iced tea on.[8]

2. Health insurance—adequate to fix the toe you break sliding down their staircase in your bare feet.[9]

3. A camera that you can operate, or a camera operator.

Mostly, though, sellers want an agent who is on their side, who will get them the highest price with the fewest repairs, who will make this life-changing event as stress free as possible. Which is why I don't believe in dual agency. How can an agent represent both the buyer and the seller in the same transaction and fulfill the requirements of agency law, to wit: "a fiduciary duty of utmost care, integrity, honesty, and loyalty in the dealings with either the Seller or the Buyers"?[10]

Those are pretty heavy responsibilities.

A seller might believe that his agent should honor his desire to get the highest sale price possible. And a

---

8    $253.75
9   Priceless
10   *Disclosure Regarding Real Estate Agency Relationships,* CAR Form AD

buyer might think that that same (dual) agent is trying to get him the lowest price. So, should a dual agent explain to them that "No, that's not the case—I'm right here in the middle, just relaying information back and forth." And collecting more commission for the disservice?

As a seller's agent, you must disclose facts, defects, and anything that could affect the value or desirability of the property. You do not have to elaborate on the ramifications of those facts. For instance, I was sitting with a client of mine while he filled out the Real Estate Transfer Disclosure Statement. He disclosed that the house had three sump pumps under it. My eyebrows raised, and he said, "That was on the disclosures *when you sold it to us, Cathy.*" My answer: "Right, but I was representing the seller, not you, and it was *your* agent's responsibility to say, 'Red flag' and encourage you to have it checked out by an expert." Which he didn't do. Had I been a dual agent back then, it would have been my duty to encourage him to have a further inspection, to open that big can of worms— and then try to jam them back in the can. I tell my sellers, "You don't want me representing both sides."

Lest anyone think that this has cost me in my career, I've heard many times, "We went with you because you won't represent both sides." And if you need a second reason, dual agency is one of the leading causes of lawsuits. The only exception I make is in leasing property.

If I don't show my rental listing and represent the tenant, it might never get leased. If tenants aren't happy, they just move; if buyers aren't happy, they sue.

Speaking of being on the seller's side, we're not doing them any favors if we sell the home before putting it on Multiple Listing. The "opportunity" will present itself: a friend at work wants to buy it for his daughter and grandkids; the painter wants it; everyone wants to get there first so *they* can get a deal. One of my neighbors stopped speaking to me because I wouldn't cooperate:

Mrs. Mom: "I want to offer $299,000 on Fred's house."

Me: "The executor of the estate is asking $399,000."

Mrs. Mom: "Well, tell him Fred liked my son and he'd want him to get a break."

Put it on the market for at least a week. If it's the listing agent's job to get market value for the seller, the best way to determine what that is is to put it on the market.

Now, brace yourself: I cut my commission on listings. What difference does it make in the grand scheme of things if I sell a $350,000 house with 2.5 percent to my side this year, and the same house next year at 3 percent of $292,000?

I hear you: "But I'm worth 3 percent!" Well, I think I'm worth more than 3 percent, but you can't put a price on great service, blood, sweat, and tears. So why haggle over one-half percent? Besides, it gets me more listings in the long run because sellers feel that I empathize with them. Other businesses have sales, why shouldn't we?

Let's Do Buyers!

But back to how to get listings so you don't become extinct: represent a lot of buyers and *farm*! We'll discuss farming in another chapter, but when you're starting out, buyers are where it's at. Happy buyers give you referrals. They stay in the neighborhoods where you work. Then life happens and they need to move. They call *you*!

Another good thing about representing buyers when you're new is that they don't typically screen agents like sellers do—probably because sellers actually sign something, and most agents don't insist on a Buyer Broker Agreement.

Buyers' agents need an additional skill set. They must have:

1. Liability insurance for when they set their notes down on a live stove in a house they're showing, and it burns to the ground.[11]

---

11   Someone else, whew.

2. Towing service

3. A car devoid of fruit flies

And patience. Because buyers really don't know what they want...that they can afford. When we bought our home, I had a wish list:

1. No composition roof

2. No overhead utility wires

3. No aluminum frame windows

I got all three—I got a comp roof, overhead wires, and aluminum windows. That's how I know that you can't count on buyers to tell you what they'll buy. You have to show them. And be patient as they tell you about their friends who got "this fabulous deal" (on a house that backs up to the freeway); that they want to buy a lot and build a house unless the "perfect" house comes along; or that they "can wait a year if we have to" during an escalating market.

I am known for my patience. My clients say, "Cathy, you are so patient." This is why I never do FaceTime—they would see me knitting a scarf and my husband rolling on the floor, pointing at me, mouthing, "Patient? *You?!*"

My second year in sales (the relevance here is that I had had one listing to date), I was the top buyer's agent in my office of thirty Realtors. I'm going to share my secret with you: *common sense*. I did not get there by running out to a listing every time a buyer called to see it. I insisted that he come to my office first. If a buyer isn't motivated enough to chat with you a while, he's either just doing "research," or he has an agent already whom he didn't call because the home is not in his price range.

When a call came in I would agree to show the home, but first I'd have my lender "run some numbers because if you decide you want to buy it, the seller won't consider your offer without a preapproval letter." And, "there may be others that you'd like, but we need to fine-tune your price range." Then the truth would start to seep out. You get this data in bits and pieces.

I would make our appointment *after* my lender chatted with the buyer, who usually went along with it because it furthered his goal—getting closer to buying that house. It furthered my goal, too.

The lender would ferret out interesting details, such as:

- "Cash? What about zero down?"
- "It was only a little bankruptcy."
- Other nuisances in the past that could derail a purchase.

After the loan officer examined the buyer from top to bottom, I'd set an appointment to meet at my office and then see the house. But had he not passed the test, I was well prepared to intelligently discuss *over the phone* what his next step should be.

Maybe, like some agents, you are afraid that if you don't run right out to the property, all eager like a puppy, you'll lose a buyer. You're right—you'll lose a good buyer while you're spinning your wheels with callers who aren't qualified. Plus, you avoid meeting axe murderers alone at a vacant listing when you prequalify buyers.

We are *always* competing. You need to convince a buyer that you are the one he wants to work with— exclusively, forever, to proceed without you is to risk great peril. You do that by taking the time to sit down in the very beginning, educate him about the process and the market, explain what you can and cannot do for him, and build a bond. It only takes an hour! (To start.)

Most agents don't do that, especially if the client was referred. They pull up a list of houses, meet at the first property, and trust that their enthusiasm about showing the buyer everything he wants to see will climax in a closed escrow. If you don't prove your professionalism in the beginning, when the going gets tough (i.e., they can't find the perfect house), they'll drop you for someone who ~~makes more promises~~ has more promise.

It's not that hard to build trust. But you have to say the right things. In the right tone of voice:

Me: "Here's the list of properties you wanted me to show you. I'm going to tell you which ones you don't want to see, because, frankly, they're bad, *very* bad, *I wouldn't touch them with a ten-foot-pole bad*, investments." It's hard to sound upbeat and ominous at once, but practice.

Mr. and Mrs. Buyer: "Really? You'd be *honest* with us?" They don't actually say that, but it's implied.

Me: "Well, of course. You can get into trouble all by yourself—you don't need an agent for that," I respond, reminding them of their vulnerability. "And your list just shrank from twenty-five to three homes," I cheerfully add.

Then I explain how we'll evaluate each property we view:

Me: "I'll tell you all the bad things and all the good things about the house. There is no 'perfect' house out there, and only you can decide what works for you. ~~You get three months~~."

Mr. and Mrs. Buyer: "Oh, good! Do you have any listings coming up in that area where you do your newsletter? That's our favorite place in the whole world."

Me: "Remember Little Red Riding Hood?"

Mr. and Mrs. Buyer: "Well, yes, but what does that have to do with your neighborhood?"

Me: "Okay, so you have a nodding acquaintance with wolves and how they can be."

Mr. and Mrs. Buyer: "Yes."

Me: "I turn into a wolf when I have a listing.[12] It would be seriously bad for you if I represented you in the purchase of one of my listings. You wouldn't like me anymore. And, as if that weren't enough (because I live for your approval), the seller would divorce me. I make a promise to all my sellers that I will never let a buyer come between us. It just wouldn't work."

Mr. and Mrs. Buyer: ~~"Wow! What integrity you have!"~~ "Oh, well, let's hope it doesn't come to that."

On that note, we go to view the ~~bait~~ listings I let them bring for our first meeting.

The first time out with a new buyer can be rather nerve-wracking. *What do you say?* Here's the good news: you only need to make enough idle chatter to fill the time between leaving the office and arriving at the first listing. Because the first house (and second, etc.) will supply all the fodder you need to chatter endlessly—to trash-talk the house. You would never do that at a friend's home, but when you're showing

---

12   See Chapter 7, Third Commandment, definition of "successful Realtor."

property, you can let all those repressed urges hang out because it will prompt your buyer to ask himself:

"Why is this person who is solely motivated by money trying to talk me out of buying this house?" It's disarming. It's positively endearing.

After a few showings, it will dawn on him that he needs to find something good about one of those homes or all those nights and weekends that he could have been playing in his new garage instead of house-hunting were for naught. And then he starts looking for reasons to buy a particular home. (This, of course, assumes that you have prescreened your client for motivation to purchase.) But the point is, he figured it out himself. You did not beat him into submission—you educated him. *You provided service!*

Your next opportunity to shine will be writing the offer. Don't go all swami on him, closing your eyes and meditating on the price. *Pull some comparable sales.* So that when the seller rejects his offer of $300,000 on her $350,000 home in an escalating market, you can say, "~~What did I tell you?~~ As a buyer, you're looking at the low comps; the seller is looking at the high ones. Shall we consider making a more realistic offer?"

Then you get into escrow, and the real fun begins: *authorities* trash the house; the lender calculates the monthly payments, complete with principal, interest, taxes, and insurance; the buyer realizes his commute just doubled. This planetary alignment makes Mercury retrograde look like a picnic. It's another reason why you must build trust from the first time you meet. Your client needs to have more confidence in your advice than that of his parents, his friends, or the mailman. They haven't seen the seventy-five houses you've shown him. They don't have a feel for what conditions are normal in that geographic area, for the prices in the current market. Everyone thinks she's an authority on real estate.

Going into the inspections, it's good to anticipate anything that might go awry before the buyer spends money on an appraisal and reports. Things that might not turn up in the disclosures...*things your client will find out from the neighbors.* But, by law, California Realtors are not required to investigate outside the perimeter of the property. We have 999 pieces of paper to shift the liability for that to the buyer.

I've been cautioned that it's not a good idea to accompany my client to the building department, the planning department, and even the title company for a signing (!), because then I'd become part of the lineup if something went wrong with whatever transpired there. Well, I can't tell you how many times being there with my client has averted disaster. I think it's worth the risk.

I perform a ritual with most of my buyers. I call it "looking for trouble." Buyers can be shy about asking nosy questions, so with them in tow I knock on doors of homes surrounding "the perfect house" and ask the neighbors: "Would you buy the same home again? Would you buy the home that's for sale? Is there anything going on in this area that we should be concerned about?"

Most of the time we get happy answers. Once, the neighbor answered:

"Are you kidding? We've been trying to get that drug dealer evicted for a year!"

Me: "What drug dealer?"

Neighbor: "The one next door!"

She was so cheerful about it that I said, "You're joking, right?"

"Hell no," she answered.

Other times we heard about an oak tree limb that fell on the house, the mold that was covered up, *the registered sex offender down the street.* All things that the sellers conveniently forgot or weren't aware of because the home had been a rental and they lived far away. If you don't go looking for trouble, it will find you.

It's very important for the buyer's agent to be at the home inspection. Physically. You. Not your assistant. Not just the home inspector and the buyer. And for sure, not you as the listing agent, almost alone with the buyer. You can't begin to discuss all the little things that turn up in the written report if you weren't there, because a lot of those issues aren't verbalized by inspectors who don't like to debate. Remember, the client is paying for your companionship. And when you're there, think! Like Nigel Newbie didn't when he and his buyer called me from a home inspection at one of my listings to ask where the vinyl floor bubble was.

Me: "Page two of the Real Estate Transfer Disclosure Statement—right where the seller said—under the kitchen table."

Nigel: "Okay! Thanks!"

I could tell from the laughter in the background that they weren't thinking about the bubble. It was big. So when the buyers moved in after escrow closed and sent over a demand that the seller pay for a new floor, we sent them another copy of page 2 of the RETDS. End of story.

The second happiest day of life with your buyer arrives: signing closing papers at the title company. The happiest day, of course, is when you present him with the key to his new home. It never ceases to amaze me when Realtors don't go to the signing. I lay awake at night before my husband and I signed papers for our first home; we would be committing to a $350-a-month mortgage!

Imagine how our clients must feel—their payments are often ten times that. They need our company.

Wonderful things happen at signings: the escrow officer tells your client how lucky she is to have a Realtor who shows up when many don't; you catch mistakes in the settlement statement (true, you can do that beforehand, but think how you'll shine when you point them out in person); you deal with hiccups before it's too late; you get free carbonated beverages. And when you're done, your client hugs you and says nice things and commits to letting you quote her to prospects. Why would you not want to go?[13]

Escrow closes. You did your job. You successfully negotiated your new BFF through the forest. You give him the key to his castle. *Now what?* There are two schools of thought on this: MyBrotherTheRealtor's and mine. My brother totally does the keeping-in-touch thing with "pop-bys" and frequent phone calls to his client base. That's. Not. Me.

On the rare occasion (usually after I've been to a seminar) that I call one or two previous clients, it's a short conversation. They already know I care about them—didn't I sign everything "XO, Cathy" when we worked together? They get my calendar every year and

---

13   Trick question.

my newsletter when I feel like doing one. But I feel awkward. I mean, if I'm calling them as a friend, isn't that an admission that I should have been doing it more frequently?[14]

Here's what they say:

"Cathy, don't worry—if we ever sell, it will be with you."

But, hey, if it works for you, do it.

In Summary

Office meetings are intended to teach, support, and inspire. Look at them as continuing ed courses—makes them go down easier. And don't miss too many—you might be forced to recite the Realtor's Pledge aloud at the next one:

> *Real estate is a fellowship of men and women who share their skills, strength, and hope with each other and their clients so that they may solve their real estate addiction and recover with a roof over their heads.*

> *There are no dues for membership, unless I count the company's split on my sales, my overhead in which the company will not participate in any way, and income taxes.*

---

14   Message to competitors: don't you dare.

The Real Estate Company is not allied with: any sect, except the California Bureau of Real Estate; politics, except those of the current administration which modifies the Business and Professions Code on a weekly basis; and does not wish to engage in any controversy, for which my errors and omissions insurance has a non-provision rider and I'll be on my own.

Our bible is the National Association of Realtors Code of Ethics. Our primary purpose is to remain viable in this market, thereby helping humanity and, incidentally, ourselves. I pledge allegiance to the Multiple Listing Service.

Put your clients first, and things work out.

Chapter 7

The Ten Commandments: Rules to Live By

There are some things that you don't want to learn by mistake. Not that I haven't made some of these mistakes myself. But if I did have big lungs, I would certainly not have violated the First Commandment:

First Commandment: No lungs!

Many years ago, MyBrotherTheRealtor came home from his first day of kindergarten and, in answer to Mom's question, "How did you like school?" he answered, "My teacher is really nice, and when she bends over you can see her lungs!" Lungs can definitely distract clients from a lack in other areas of competence, for a while.

I always accompany my clients to their signings at the title company. In walked the escrow officer (fifteen minutes late) with nails to here and a blouse to there. Whenever the couple, sitting across from her, asked a question, she stood up, bent over, and pointed to the line item which she could easily have touched, sitting down, with one of those fingernails. Mr. Seller probably wouldn't have caught it if she had charged for the view, but his wife and I noticed the $30,000 error she made on their net proceeds.

Second Commandment: Be honest

Honesty is always appropriate. Except where a white lie is prudent. Like when Animal Control wants you to rat on your client's dog that had all its shots but nipped puppy daddy's leg in his exuberance at seeing you—why would I want to sentence that puppy to jail?

Or someone who has her home listed with another agent calls to borrow your garage sale signs and asks, "Oh, by the way, can you drop them at my house?" It's OK to lie.

Third Commandment: Enthuse

To be a successful Realtor, it's helpful to be type A, anal retentive, a wolf (they're not all bad) in sheep's clothes who protects her own fiercely, the iron fist in a velvet glove—Attila the Honey—with a warm and fuzzy smile.

You must display enthusiasm. I always try to have a smile in my voice, so first thing in the morning I reach for my bottle of caffeine pills, grind one up with a mortar and pestle, and down it in juice. I call it "artificial enthusiasm."

And at the end of the day, after dodging bullets, preventing train wrecks, and saving marriages, it's OK to have a "wine emergency." I have those frequently, but I know I'm not an alcoholic because many nights I must do without for fear of getting arrested on the way to an appointment.

Fourth Commandment: Observe the Golden Rule

Because God (or the other agent) will get you. Like the time my lifelong friend, the loan officer, called me.

Charlie: "Would you be upset if I listed my house with Alice the Agent?"

Me:

Charlie: "Well, she told me that if I didn't list my house with her, her client wouldn't be inclined to accept my offer."

Me (regaining my composure): "You didn't."

Charlie: "I told her I had promised to list it with you. She said you wouldn't mind."

Me: "Why would I mind, Charlie? We go back decades. I hired you when you changed careers. I've referred business to you for years. You get my bourbon fudge at Christmas. Why would I be upset that you sold out our friendship?"

Charlie: "Is it too late?"

Me: "Unlike buying a used car, which she's trying to sell you, there's no cooling off period with real estate contracts. However, there is a little something you can do to make me feel better. You can call Alice up, tell her that she interfered in an agency relationship, and that I would like a 50 percent referral fee."

And he did! And Alice knew that had she not agreed, I could have taken her to the Board of Realtors and probably taken her whole commission.

Which, sadly, I had to do to Barry the Broker. Apropos of saving some time for clients who help me pay my bills, I thoroughly screen callers whose employers move them to my area. More times than not, they have a relocation package that requires the employer to choose the real estate agent to represent the employee. For which the employer gets half the commission and doubles the agent's paperwork.

"Steve" cleared all my hurdles. He had a narrow window of time for his purchase, so we spent hours and hours together, popping in and out of houses, Starbucks, and gas stations until we found the perfect house. We discussed offer strategy, I quizzed the listing agent, I wrote a purchase contract. And then, Steve disappeared!

He didn't return my friendly phone calls. He didn't answer my e-mails. He didn't sign the contract I had written. The perfect house, though, went pending two days later, with Barry the Broker representing the buyer.

So I called the listing agent, who was very confused at this point because she thought I was Steve's agent. So did I. Then I called Barry, who had probably sicced Steve on me to do his legwork, and told him that I would accept "only" a 25 percent referral fee, to be nice, because according to our Multiple Listing Service Code, I was the "procuring cause," and therefore, entitled to the whole commission.

I guess Steve and Barry thought I would go away if they ignored me, but no. My righteous indignation had been aroused, so I took Barry to the Board and won his whole commission. It's always important to be nice.

Fifth Commandment: Do not engage

I learned this from MyHusbandTheEngineer. He can stand amazingly still, with a faraway look on his face, while someone (not me) delivers the most challenging assault to his ~~patience~~ problem-solving ability. Something happens when he does this:

- The other person solves the problem himself while rattling on, or
- The other person hears himself talking and realizes how unreasonable he's being, or
- The other person runs out of breath, and the silence is deafening.

I have adapted this strategy to real estate. My challenges usually come to me over the phone, so I must convert the gaze into words. I say, "Uh huh. Ummmmm. I see." Mostly I let the other person talk. If I don't get one of the results above, I tell the caller that I need to process the information and will get back to him that evening. And then I do. By that time, he's usually figured it out himself. I could have told him the solution earlier in the day, but he wouldn't have been ready to hear it. Sometimes you have to let the balloon deflate.

Sixth Commandment: Look like you care

It gets you halfway there. I must have missed the memo about shorts. Once, a homeowner greeted my client (clad in her spandex biking pants) and me at the door with "Which one of you is the Realtor?" Okay...

Seventh Commandment: Be yourself

When I had my last business photo taken, the photographer said, "There, that ought to do you for another ten years." He was not complimenting me on my youthful preservation; rather, he was alluding to Realtors' propensity to use the same photo for the rest of their professional lives. I beat his estimate—mine lasted fifteen years, and the only thing that changed was my hairstyle... that I could detect.

I was passing out newsletters in my geographic farm a while back, and an elderly gentleman took one, looked at it, looked at me, squinted, and asked in a dubious voice, "Is this you?"

"Yes," I answered. "On a good day."

And in these times male agents, especially, need to resemble their photos if they want to get through the homeowner's door.

Eighth Commandment: Don't look dumb

It's natural to want to present your best face. But if you would rather be an attorney than a real estate appraiser, do not call yourself an "appraiser at real estate," as one of my associates in Idaho did. Just go be a lawyer. And for heaven's sake, don't name your hydroplane speedboat "Your 6 percent." I think that agent was the same one whose outgoing phone message was "Hi, this is Susie. I'm out making a killing in real estate. Leave your name and number and I'll get back to ya." (I couldn't make this stuff up.)

I don't understand why Realtors have to advertise how much they earn when other professionals don't. I can see listing the number of homes we've sold, although doctors don't list the number of body parts they've replaced; the public does need to have some means of measuring our success, but really...

Ninth Commandment: Something to do with cars

Cars bore me to distraction. Before I became a Realtor, mine had fruit flies in it. But since real estate agents have to put other people in their cars, keep them tidy, and look successful, I was forced to clean up my act. My first real estate car was a Honda Accord. I learned that no matter how modest an image you project, you can't click with everyone. Like the fellow who said, "It must be nice to be able to afford a new Accord."

An Accord will pass as successful if it's brand new. Every year its ability to assure potential clients of your worthiness depreciates. Next, I was forced to trade my five-year-old Accord in on an Acura when I got tired of hearing (only from men) words to this effect:

Mr. Buyer: "We're riding in this?"

Me: Smile. Nod.

Mr. Buyer: (silence)

Some of them even noticed the scratches on my bumpers.

Other agents "get it" faster. Like Susie, who always wanted to quit her county job and go into real estate. She stopped by a while back, so excited, to say that she had "started (her) real estate career!"

I said, "Oh, wow, you passed the exam?"

"No." She grinned. "I got me my Mercedes!"

Tenth Commandment: Stop talking

There are two times when you should not talk: when you're talking to a client on the phone, and when you're talking to a client face-to-face. Because, let's admit it, they don't want to hear about *us*. They want us to listen to *them*. Which is only fair—they're paying.

So just say enough to prime the pump, to get them going. And then, if you're on the phone, you can pick up your knitting and make a scarf. Because that's about how much time you should devote to *listening*. I've considered giving the longest scarves to the corresponding clients but thought better of it.

Chatting in person calls for another skill set: body language. Serious listening can induce drowsiness. As can my didactic preaching, so I'm not going to dwell on this. But you know what I'm saying here.

I once took another broker in my office with me to a listing presentation in a town where I had few listings, because he had been a longtime resident there and knew *everything* about it. (It's true—he said so, repeatedly.) He also knew everything about skiing, his kids' palatial home in Silicon Valley, and politics. It was really hard to tear

~~him~~ ourselves away. The next day the homeowners called me to say, "If we decide to go with you, whatever you do, don't bring him back."

Thou shalt use common sense.

CHAPTER 8

It's Always the Realtor's Fault. Avoid Those Litigious Moments

I come by feelings of guilt naturally—I am the oldest of four siblings and attended Catechism class religiously. A guilty conscience is easier to assuage than a legal verdict of guilty, but I strive to avoid both. So when a client suggests that I risk everything to keep his business, I disengage.

Like the day I had to give back a listing—tragic. Not so much for me, but for my client whose son had committed suicide in their basement, and she didn't believe that even though it had happened five years before, they still had to disclose it.

Mrs. Bereaved: "But you said the law about disclosing a death on the property was three years."

Me: "Yes, but it also says you have to disclose any material fact that could affect the value or desirability of the property. You must realize that just being in the basement where that happened is going to unnerve some potential buyers?"

Mrs. Bereaved: "But if we don't tell them, they won't know."

Me: "Don't you think that's the first thing your neighbors will tell them after they move in?"

And so, we hugged and parted company.

A Realtor's job is to create excitement without misrepresenting the property. And since we have a fiduciary duty to protect our clients from themselves, we must educate them about what is important to disclose. My attorney would argue that I'm not responsible for information that my clients don't share with me, but I'll still get named in the lawsuit. So being proactive, asking questions, and a little mind-reading can spare everyone grief.

Me: "Never had any issues with the agricultural land behind you?"

Mrs. Country Property Owner: "Nooooooooooo. Welllllllll, maybe once in a while a cow bumps the fence."

Mr. Country Property Owner: "Bumps the fence?! They knock it over and eat our flowers!"

Some people might think that it's cute to see cows grazing at their windows. But many buyers would use this little detail, if undisclosed, to extort money from the seller (and the agent) after escrow closes.

So everything our clients tell us in casual conversation, in an e-mail, at the grocery store—if it's something that could concern a buyer we'd better make a note, because we have just become an accessory to the potential crime of omission. In Realtor parlance, the client has just *shifted the liability*. If they forget to put it on the disclosures their fallback is, "We told our agent." If you are the listing agent this only need concern you up until the close of escrow. I was so relieved to learn that the DEA shoot-out that happened next door to a listing of mine occurred at 2:00 p.m. on the day we closed escrow at 10 a.m.

I do not lose any sleep over this because I fall into bed every night, bone tired. Rather, it causes me to sit bolt upright in bed at three in the morning, in a cold sweat, asking myself after an escrow closes: "Did we put that in the disclosures?"

It's our job to know contractors. And referring one puts us in the middle if the job is botched and we neglected to check whether his state license is active or if he's bonded and insured—or if he's not, in which case we must tell the homeowner to "proceed at your own risk." What a relief it was to learn that the contractor who installed three doggie doors with the flaps going sideways, not up and down, at Mrs. Jones's home was not someone I had referred.

In a very helpful article about how to stay in real estate and out of trouble, Phoenix, Arizona, broker/defense attorney and former administrative law judge Robert Bass cautions that "the best way to avoid making a misrepresentation is to make no representations at all. In practice, you can learn to easily avoid answering almost any question...You can just say 'I don't know.'"

But too many of these, and your client may turn to you and ask, "What *do* you know?" (And why did I hire you?) Mr. Bass would respond, "Well, I do know how to help you find the most qualified person to answer your questions; that way we know you can rely on what the expert tells you." In other words, let the expert make the representation.

I remind myself that getting out of bed in the morning subjects me to risk.

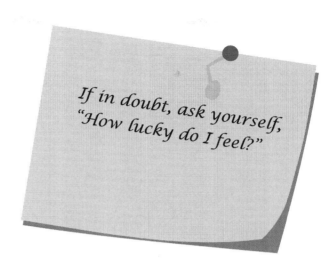

If in doubt, ask yourself,
"How lucky do I feel?"

Chapter 9

Lawyers–Friendly and Otherwise. More Litigation Avoidance

According to the 2013 Avery Index of law firms, California has approximately one lawyer per thousand residents, which is fewer than the ratio of state-licensed real estate practitioners to normal people (one per 92). With these odds, you'd think Realtors would be safe. But, no sirree, we are not! Why, I would liken at least one of those lawyers to a cannibal or, at the risk of maligning wolves, a wolf.

I met my Stanford-educated, charming, smooth-talking (former) attorney during an escrow. I was not being sued and my clients, a brother and sister who had just inherited the family home, did not deserve to be sued. But sued they were by their half-sister whose biological dad and stepmother had bought her out of her inheritance years earlier, just to make her go away. She wanted more.

BadSister got herself a better lawyer than Mom and Dad had, and he found a loophole. She ended up with another half of the house. And the poor brother and sister had to divide up the remaining half among themselves— and their lawyer.

But how could I be mad at BadSister's attorney? He was just doing his job—exceedingly well. Wow, I thought. I must share this gem with my clients (and get a little reciprocity going here). So I referred him far and wide.

Needless to say, a leopard does not change his spots; I became prey, too. Next thing I knew, *he* was selling *my* clients' homes. So now I have MyNewLawyer, who has *my* best interests at heart. As wonderful as he is, though, I try to avoid needing his services—as a defendant.

It's obvious when another agent doesn't have good legal counsel (or common sense). Like Susie Agent whom MyNewLawyer would have told that:

- if an investor canceled a purchase because his inspector told him verbally that the house is riddled with mold (a fact that Susie's seller denied),

- and that investor continues to live on the same

street as that house,

- and you try (and succeed) to resell it without disclosing that fact because "it's not in writing,"

then that investor might tell everyone around that your seller (and you) committed fraud.

Actually, MyNewLawyer would probably have said, *"What were you thinking?!"*

As a Realtor you must never stop thinking. Paranoia is a good quality to cultivate. It serves you well when, for example, you get a phone call from a sweet young thing with a heavy foreign accent who tries to talk you out of showing her your two-bedroom rental listing because, well, you'll see:

Ms. Shill: "I want to rent your house."

Cautious me: "Wouldn't you like to see it first?"

Ms. Shill: "Oh! You would show it to me?! I have lots of kids and no husband and no money."

Cautious me: "Perfect! When would you like to meet me there?"

Ms. Shill: "Oh! I don't know. I have to ask my lawyer." (Babble, babble, babble.) "Never mind."

Yes, you should screen your showings. But toodling over to that property would cost less than the lawsuit her starving lawyer had in mind.

I would love to engage in online neighborhood gossip and attend homeowners' meetings. But if I did, everything I heard that could possibly be construed as affecting the value or desirability of any home in my neighborhood would become a disclosure item for me. Even if it's a rumor. I'd have to disclose the rumor and narrate that "I did not verify the information but if buyer is concerned, buyer should investigate." Ridiculous, you say. Yes, but, again, better than a lawsuit. Just nip it in the bud.

And lawyers are why you want to *anticipate* anything that might go wrong. Because if they can't get you on a law, they'll get you on fiduciary duty. I know my lovely repeat customer, Mr. Spec, thought I was crazy stomping through the weeds on the acre lot belonging to a hundred-year-old ranch house he was considering buying:

Mr. Spec: "What are you doing?"

Me: "Oh, just looking for a needle in a haystack."

Which was revealed to us upon questioning the neighbor (this was an estate sale, and the owner wasn't alive to disclose anything) who remembered the previous owner having a gas tank and pump installed during World War II so that he'd have enough fuel to run his farm equipment. And Mr. Spec was able to stick the estate (not me) with removal of that toxic little tank. I know, again, ridiculous. But, get a good lawyer and...

If you are a new agent, don't let any of this scare you. God protects the innocent. Just be sure you stay innocent.

Chapter 10

The Pitfalls of Excessive Success

The Master said, "If your conduct is determined solely by considerations of profit you will arouse great resentment."

— Confucius

We have always known that heedless self-interest was bad morals; we now know that it is bad economics.

— Franklin D. Roosevelt

One day I was busily web-searching for artsy images to decorate a real estate flyer for the one and only listing that was the product of my first eleven months in the biz. My husband, John, entered my sanctuary:

"If you expect to list more than one house a year, you need to step away from the computer," he proffered.

Larry Knapp, then president of Coldwell Banker, had postulated a similar theory: "Business is done nose to nose and toes to toes."

I was more comfortable sponging—absorbing everything real estate and staying out of sight. A nice thing about animals of the sponge species is that they don't have nervous systems so they can't experience rejection. I could live there. But I'd have to be satisfied with eating plankton unless John would accept my metamorphosis. Which is why he violated my sanctuary that day.

"We need to justify this exercise to the IRS," John said.

"Success happens slowly. Let's not rush it," I said.

I reminded him of some monumental backfires when agents got *too successful*. Like the listing king who built his home on the hill in the middle of his farm and lost his serfdom. And the home warranty rep who blogged about all her trips to Europe. Poof—gone! Good lessons.

"You have a way to go before that happens," John commented.

Eventually my business increased, despite my purchasing an Acura, and I needed help. Potential clients asked me if was too busy for them; hiring an assistant could definitely send that message. I know, I know—most professionals have someone in the back office. But let's face it—our clients want to feel like they're special, Number One, the *only* one. They acknowledge that we need to sell more than one house at a time, but can't we do that after theirs is sold and closed? And take vacations during someone else's escrow? I had to get past my hang-up and hire somebody to deal with the increasing paperwork.

Janie was supposed to put together disclosure packages for me, answer the phone, and log significant escrow events. I'd do the "ear-to-ear" client contact myself. I quickly discovered that it was better to blame myself when the main disclosure document was missing at a client meeting; that my answering machine said "Cathy's not in" more pleasantly than Janie did; and that "escrow closing" and "pay day" were not synonymous in her book. When she announced that she had saved up all her coffee breaks for the week and was not coming in on Friday, I decided that Janie would be happier staying at home where her mind was most of the time, anyway.

I'd been forced to get even more organized when I hired her, so it wasn't too big a stretch to just do it myself.

But as business increased I felt that I was losing the personal touch, so I hired Maxie. Maxie informed me that the twenty hours a week she insisted be worked from her home would be chosen by her, probably wouldn't include Mondays or Fridays, may be in the middle of the night depending on her sleep habits, and that if I didn't keep her busy enough to fill twenty hours I would still pay her for twenty hours. OK. Fair enough. Although I did think accruing vacation time for part-time work was pushing it. But when she decided she didn't want to do what I asked of her to fill the time because it was "boring," I was back on my own again.

I had a heart-to-heart with myself—you talk to yourself a lot in real estate. It's good to wear a Bluetooth so when you're doing this as you walk down the street people will give you the benefit of the doubt. I said, "Self, it's obvious that what makes you happiest is being appreciated. You only need enough income to balance that with your overhead and a little profit to justify this exercise to your husband and the IRS." So now I have no assistance.

I'm not saying that some agents can't handle dozens of escrows at a time, hold hands like an octopus, and nurse a baby. But when an agent says to one of her listing clients who happens to call when her assistant is on the other two phone lines, "Excuse me, I'm really busy, but do I know you?" (that agent's client relisted with me), well, the public gets the message.

Success is a hard look to master.

Check the mirror.

PART III – IN THE TRENCHES

Chapter 11

Let's Just Say the Grass Is Green on the Other Side of the Fence

I remember the *Aha!* moment vividly: Standing at my kitchen sink, looking out the window, across the barren lot behind my house, thinking, "This is all there is." My sixth month in Idaho. Nothing could have prepared me for the vacuum that a Bay Area transplant experiences when relocating to, well, someplace else. Especially Idaho.

I think Mark Twain said the longest ten years he ever spent were his two months in Idaho. No? Well, he would have had he lived there. My real-estate-oriented family and I thought Idaho would be a great investment opportunity and made a rather irreversible move by selling everything we owned in California and buying twice as many ~~headaches~~ rentals in our new homeland.

I learned really fast that there are worse things than earthquakes, commute traffic, and high prices.

Clients do similarly silly things, like relocate when *you* know it's not in their best interest. If you care about them, tell them that the grass is greener elsewhere because the leach lines leak; that food is cheaper because they ship the good stuff to places where people can pay more for it; that in the states where you need it most you can't buy wine at the grocery store.

But if they insist, suggest they rent for a while first. That's what Oma and Opa should have done when their daughter, Rising Star, got a marvelous promotion to Florida and informed them that she was taking their grandchildren with her.

Me: "What will you do if she gets transferred again?"

Oma: "Oh, no, this is permanent."

Me: "Like the last ones."

Opa: "She wouldn't move the kids again—school."

Grandchildren render grandparents incapable of making rational decisions. I never heard from them again, but I did learn through the grapevine that Rising Star performed so well in her new capacity that she was promoted yet again, to New York.

She was so wonderful there that the company subsidized her housing but not Oma's and Opa's, who by that point were too exhausted to ship their oxygen equipment and hospital bed to the big city, anyway, so the high price of housing was a moot issue. I ask you: is it better to be stranded back home in California with its earthquakes or in Florida with hurricanes and alligators?

As Kermit the Frog said, "It's not easy being green." A Realtor must soldier on like a tadpole swimming upstream, trying to impart her learned wisdom and unwelcome facts to a clientele resolute in making what she believes could be the worst decision of their lives. Sometimes I just want to ~~shout~~ respectfully submit, "You'll be sorry."

If you live in an area that's got buildable land, another challenge Realtors face is the "move-up" buyer who shouldn't. Occasionally, they ask for your opinion:

Mr. Boomer: "I'm not so sure about this, but Mrs. B really wants one of those brand new McMansions in Timber Buck II."

Me: "That development that would extend your commute by an hour?"

Mrs. Boomer: "Well, only ~~if he makes it~~ until retirement."

Me: "Retirement! Yes! You do want to do that, don't you?"

And then a discussion ensues about making a monthly $4,000 mortgage payment well into their eighties, how likely his employer is to keep him laying carpet until then, and other annoying considerations that cause them to stop me in my tracks with, "Well, we already made a down payment on it."

You know that if you argue they'll just go with another Realtor who may not be as compassionate, so you accept the listing, vowing to make the process as humane as possible—they'll need to conserve their strength for the ordeal of owning the mini-mansion. It's the merciful thing to do.

Accept with serenity the things that cannot be changed.

Chapter 12

My Biggest Challenge. Listen Between the Lines

My greatest challenge in real estate is people who don't "get it." I'm sure my CPA says the same thing about me.

Sales is all about educating the client. Think of yourself as the teacher in a class with a lot of remedial readers. Take the Henrys.

Mr. Henry: "Why did you have to go and put it on our listing that we have to close by October 31 because of capital gains?"

Me: "You would rather get into escrow, have some unforeseen postponement happen and hear me say 'Surprise! You have to close anyway'?" And pay capital gains or get sued for specific performance? This is not

Burger King—you can't always have it your way in real estate.

The ones I feel sorry for, though, are the folks who have a hard time remembering things (such as their marital status) or who rehydrate with alcohol:

Mrs. Alfred: "I want to buy a house with you."

Me: "Is Al going with you?"

Mrs. Alfred: "No. I'm not going to tell him."

I gently explain to her that at some point we'll have to mention this to Al (and get his signature on a sales contract from whence the money for her purchase would need to come), and even if it all fell into place, "He'd miss you."

Mrs. Al: "I guess I should just stay here, huh?"

I would need to refresh her memory several times afterward. Al and their son were most appreciative.

Sometimes there isn't a spouse, and the kids aren't around...until their inheritance is in jeopardy.

Helen: "I want to move."

Me: (Observing the waist-high weeds in her backyard, the piles of dishes in the sink, her walker, and the empty vodka bottles in the trash.) "Where would you go?"

Helen: "Oh, I'd travel."

Me: "Have you talked to the kids about this?"

Helen: "They don't need to know."

Unfortunately, I did not have contact information for them, and the neighbors told me that they rarely came around. But I checked in regularly. Eventually, I saw another company's sign in the yard—probably the kids' Realtor's. I just hope they spent their inheritance on good care for Mom.

Then there are the young 'uns, focused on the fairy-tale end result, oblivious to all the hazards along the way, of which you, their agent, repeatedly, redundantly, remind them.

Me: "The house is on a septic tank. You can't replace it per the county. You would need to plan on spending $30,000 to change over to sewer."

Penelope: "Oh, we know it's old."

Me: "It's 55 years old, redwood, and can't even be repaired per the County because they won't give you a building permit. Plus, you can't add the second bath you need for your family of six, and...*what's that smell?*"

Mr. Penelope: "Oh, my grandfather built septic tanks, and he never got a permit."

Me: "Those were the good ol' days. Gone."

Penelope: "It would only cost $5,000 to replace it."

Me: ~~Were you listening?!~~ "No, it was $30,000, to *convert*. You can't replace it."

Time to call in the reinforcements. Mom and Dad accompanied us to the County Planning Department, the Water District, the Flood Zone Agency (yes, that too), Engineering, and Environmental Health. We communicated so often I set up an e-mail group for the family. The kids bought the property anyway, but they're now authorities on septic tanks.

While my primary objective is to keep my clients out of trouble, protecting my ~~bottom~~ bottom line is every bit as important to me. Once a client said to me, "You're just trying to protect yourself." Well, no. I look at protecting myself as a byproduct of protecting *them*. But one way or another, *we* are going to be protected.

Occasionally you'll encounter a client who wants to "slip one by" and let the agent take the hit. I don't think the Swizzles had the capacity to grasp the consequences of representing their little homestead as subdividable. So I took them to the Building Department.

Nice building inspector: "Sorry, folks, not enough land to accommodate setbacks for two lots and access to the back lot. And you'd have to jack the house up and move it 30 feet to the side to have a buildable site even if there was enough room."

Me: "Which, Mr. Swizzle, considering the cost to move it and install a new foundation would be prohibitive, not to mention diminishing the lot value; two small lots are not twice as valuable as the original big lot."

I could hear the gears grinding in Mr. Swizzle's head.

Nice building inspector: "And there would be no street access to a rear lot."

Mr. Swizzle: "There's back access! I use it all the time."

Me: "You mean the canal easement with the 'No Trespassing' sign behind your house?"

Then we put the house on the market.

Alice Agent: "Hi! I'm bringing in an offer $100,000 over asking. Can you present now?"

Me: "And why, may I ask, did you write so high?"

Alice Agent: "Well, because you have it underpriced! The lot can be split!"

Me: "Let me guess..."

So I called Mr. Swizzle.

"Remember what the city said about splitting the lot?"

Mr. Swizzle: "I know it can be split!"

Me: "Why don't you and I go back to the city and explain to them the extenuating circumstances that would make your lot dividable. OK?"

So we return to the Building Department where all of Mr. Swizzle's objections are overruled, and he promises to be honest and truthful in his representations to every single real estate agent and prospective buyer who sets foot on his unsubdividable lot.

And then I get another $100,000 over asking price offer. Which brings me to the next chapter and the perfect storm.

Certain sellers need to be debriefed after every showing.

Chapter 13

The Competition.
Excellence Is an Attitude

Because good Realtors make selling real estate look like there's nothing to it, and they make a living at it, the profession attracts some people who excel at not doing too much. True, you have to pass an exam, but you can be a good test-taker and pass without studying the Code of Ethics or proper procedures. And until a few years ago, you could get a broker's license without any real estate sales experience if you had a four-year college degree.

Occasionally, you run into one of those brokers who managed to bypass all that tedious training you get when you join an established company. Such was Barbie the Broker.

Barbie: "Hi, Cathy! I just sold your listing!" is what I thought I heard through my Vicodin-induced stupor one hour after a root canal.

Me: "Oh, great. Send the contract over and I'll present it when I come back to earth."

Barbie: "Your clients said you weren't available today, so I took it over and had them sign it already."

Me: "You did *WHAT?!*" Please, God, don't let it be the Swizzles' listing. It was.

I had my husband drive me over to their home, where Mr. Swizzle was grinning from ear to ear because, "I just sold the house myself, so you should reduce the commission!" And, the cherry on top—"I got $100,000 over asking!"

It's less time-consuming to build a house from scratch than it is to remodel a fixer-upper. The same tenet applies to undoing a transaction that should never have happened in the first place. Five addenda plus a letter citing passages from the Agency Relationships section of the Code of Ethics, a copy of the zoning ordinance pertaining to lot splits, and the potential of having to appear before the Ethics Committee of the Board of Realtors induced Barbie to have her clients rescind their offer.

Barbie and the Swizzles were meant for each other. Unfortunately, I was the third wheel.

There are many fine agents out there who make me proud to be a Realtor. And that's why the others are startling by comparison. For instance:

Angela Agent: "Calling about your listing on Heavenly Street. Can you describe the home to me in detail?"

Me: "I went into ~~excruciating~~ detail on the Multiple Listing and the flyer is attached."

Angela Agent: "But what's the street like? How close is it to the drug house? Help me here. My clients don't think I'm doing my job."

Me: "Just think how impressed they'll be when you spend some money on gas and drive over to preview it."

And then, there was my one-acre lot listing in the hills, about which I explicitly explained with elaborate exactitude that there was *no way* the lot could be split, only to be asked by an agent with her client in tow:

"My client here is going to write an offer on this. What does R-6 mean?"

Me: "You don't know?"

Agent: "No."

I think her only association with the number 6 was the commission. Imagine her surprise when she learned that a simple phone call to the county (or me) would have informed her that the minimum lot size for this property was 6,000 square feet, but because of the slope it couldn't be split into buildable lots. Could have saved her a trip out to the property, too.

Also swimming in the pool of competitors are the sons and daughters with parents nearing retirement age who get their real estate license to save Mom and Dad the commission. Or retirees who want to "dabble" in real estate. Real estate is the kind of thing that you should tiptoe into, gradually immersing yourself in the hundreds of forms and "thou shalt nots" you need to be aware of. It helps if you started in the 1970s.

When my mom began her real estate career, the purchase contract was one page (it's now ten), there was no disclosure law (the basic disclosure package today is about 75 pages, unless it's a condo or planned unit development—then it's 275 pages), and there are dozens more forms that come in handy if the situation, which you'd better be able to recognize, presents itself.

It would be so much easier if we could just do everything for the client—fill out all the forms, negotiate, get their signatures at the beginning and the end—"Here's your house; here's your money!" I know what my sellers want: the highest price with the minimum repairs. My buyers want the lowest price and the maximum repairs. I get it. I'll be fighting tooth and nail for them, regardless of how involved they are. My favorite thing in the whole world is when my client says; "I trust you, what would you do? Where do I sign?" *Just let me do it!*

Although...the more involved they are, the less likely they'll be to become Realtors themselves, thereby discouraging more competition. "I thought I'd want to sell real estate until now," they often say halfway through escrow. "How can you stand doing this?" Music to my ears!

"Excellence is not a skill. It is an attitude."

Ralph Marsten

Chapter 14

The "Tedious," aka the Real Estate Transfer Disclosure Statement (TDS)

There are few points during a real estate transaction when your physical presence is actually required. But that does not mean that you shouldn't be working feverishly behind the scenes doing that 95 percent of the work your client never witnesses.

"Lulubelle" didn't know that. The former Miss South Carolina, whose looks and charm assured her a brilliant career in sales (*if she'd just do the work*), got herself a listing early on. A new agent myself, I'd occasionally ask her how it was going, and she'd glow in all her pulchritude and say, "Great!" And it was (for her) until the day escrow was supposed to close...and our heretofore mild-mannered office manager came storming out of his office and ordered her into it.

Lulubelle didn't realize that she was the one who was supposed to order the pest inspection and coordinate the repairs; that she was supposed to get all the disclosures signed; that she was supposed to, well, *do something.* And her seller was not happy about that misunderstanding. Or the fact that since his escrow would not be closing for at least another week, he couldn't purchase the home that he himself had made a contingent offer on and lined up a mover for...a place to put his eight-months-pregnant wife.

Our manager was worried about being sued because, as you know, it's always the Realtor's fault, and in this case it really was. So I think this cost Lulubelle her commission. The escrow did eventually close; our manager was very proactive.

Lulubelle left the business shortly after that, so my inquisitive mind fixated on a more experienced agent, a former professional ballplayer who seemed to have no trouble dealing with the stacks and stacks of documents that agents need to originate and get signed by all parties—and be conversant in their content. I could learn from him, I thought. Here's what I learned: there's a reason why all those forms have "Date signed" on them.

And that date should not be the same on all those papers. And, for certain, it shouldn't be two days before escrow closes. And you can get into a lot of trouble when it catches up with you. He left, too.

There is just no way around paperwork in real estate. You'd better like it. My blog, www.ALittleBitOff. net, attests to the fact that I am, well...I love paperwork. I love checking completed forms off of my list. I love it when the last "i" is dotted and the last "t" is crossed out and initialed, or whatever.

There are roughly one million forms in the California Association of Realtors library, which are there for the sole purpose of ~~discouraging potential new agents from entering the business~~ helping Realtors and clients cover all our litigious bases.

I recommend the total immersion method of familiarizing yourself with these documents. Tell your significant other, your day-job employer, the IRS, everybody, that there will be a one-month interruption in your performance of family duties and income stream while you closet yourself with this stack of forms. You may then be reasonably familiar enough with them to *practice* real estate.

Once you become familiar with the disclosures, sit down with your client and break it to him gently that now it's his turn. He will ask why he should take a week's vacation to fill them out. You answer:

"Because civilization is crumbling faster than your house and the lawyers need billable hours."

The three most important words in real estate are "disclose, disclose, disclose," not "location, location, location." The disclosures are your Get Out of Jail Free card, and filling them out with your client is, I believe, part of that 5 percent of the time when your physical presence is required.

An agent I know once remarked, "If I gave each of my clients a fax machine, I'd never have to see them again." Do not do that with the disclosures. Alternatively, you could have your assistant e-mail the package to your client. Neither of these solutions is prudent. If you weren't holding his ~~pen~~ other hand as he filled them out, observing what he wrote like a hawk, watching him exchange furtive glances with his wife, you could miss something that might be conspicuous by its absence later—in court.

The origin of the first statutorily required disclosure form can be traced back to a 1984 court case, *Easton vs. Strassburger*, in which it was found that real estate agents must not only disclose material defects that they know about, but ones that they *should* know about. I did not make this up. I swear. It's right there in California Civil Code Section 2079(a).

This resulted in creation of the Real Estate Transfer Disclosure Statement, which we in the biz refer to by the acronym "TDS," which rhymes with "tedious," and which for purposes of this discussion will be referred to as "The Tedious."

Since what Realtors *should* know about is pretty subjective, and God help us if it comes to a trial by jury of our peers, I have created a multipurpose, all-encompassing, this-will-get-you-into-heaven-no-matter-what "Tedious." I share the use of this copyrighted material with you as a bonus for buying my book. The following page is a sample.

The Real Estate Transfer Disclosure Statement—Just do it.

CALIFORNIA
ASSOCIATION
OF REALTORS NOT®

The Tedious
(California Civil Code 999∞)
(C.A.R.N. Form TT)

THIS DISCLOSURE STATEMENT CONCERNS THE REAL PROPERTY SITUATED IN THE
CITY OF _____, COUNTY OF _____
STATE OF CALIFORNIA,DESCRIBED AS _____
AS OF (date) _____ It concerns:

- The house and every nut, screw, bolt, fixture, and bit of construction material within it and every appurtenance to it;
- The land above, around, and beneath the foundation;
- And everything overhead and below it;
- Seller is advised that statements made in this document are to be taken as seriously as marriage vows and must be at least that honest and truthful. Upon signing The Tedious, Seller and Buyer acknowledge receipt of information that they could use against each other in a court of law. Seller will disclose everything that ever happened on/above/below/to this property and every thought that he, or any member of his family, or guest, has had as it pertains to this property and anything and anyone within its boundaries that Seller is aware of.

Part I: Simplified Coordinating Disclosures:
1. Agency Disclosure: The Seller's agent works for the Seller.The Buyer's agent works for the Buyer.
2. Carbon Monoxide Disclosure: If it doesn't have one, get one.
3. Smoke Detector Disclosure: If it doesn't have them, get them. In every room except the kitchen—better safe than sorry.
4. Water Heater Disclosure: If it isn't strapped, strap it—read the directions.
5. Natural Hazards Disclosure: Current natural hazards reports are attached and are subject to change due to global warming, shifting tectonic plates, and politics.

Part II: Circle the correct answer:
1. Any deaths on the property in the past three years? Yes/No
2. Earthquakes? Yes/No
3. Federal & State Tax Withholding: I am/am not a U.S. Citizen. My tax ID number is:_____
4. Lead-based paint? Yes/No/Maybe

Part III: Other information that Seller deems pertinent to this sale:

(Include anything that might concern the pickiest buyer) _____
_____
_____

Part IV: The attached 850 forms are included for situations that may arise and run with the deed in perpetuity.
Signed: _____ Date: _____

Signed: _____ Date: _____

Part V: Agent's Disclosure: *I certify that I don't know if the sellers are telling the truth, but I hope so because they are very nice people who don't deserve to be sued. Please see attached "Agent's Inspection Checklist."*

Signed: _____ Date: _____

Copyright © 2014, California Association of Realtors Not®,Inc.

THE TEDIOUS (TT PAGE 1of 1)

Chapter 15

Short Sale, Long Story. Comic Interlude

Why do we not love short sales? (*Oh, be quiet if you do.*) Because, well, here's what I had to do for my last, *I swear to God*, short sale: Everything!

- Photograph, inventory, and e-mail to the daughter—who conveniently resided in Europe—details on every single piece of personal property (which Mom left a houseful of) that could possibly have any value.

- Call out three consignment places to appraise the valuables (of course, they couldn't all agree on what was valuable and what was not, so there were three lists instead of one, but you know how important it is to get three of everything).

- Personally take all the silverware to another consignment shop which went out of business a month later before paying my client. Fortunately, the owner was married to a loan officer I know, so I could shame him into paying up—two months later.

- Run interference between daughter and mother, who wanted to know why we were selling her "Tiffany" lamp, etc., for "peanuts."

- Be there for the pickup by the highest bidding shop.

- Call out and be there for the Salvation Army to get what little they'd take.

- Get the trash-out guy to remove the rest.

- Have Merry Maids, the window cleaner, carpet installer, and painter do their thing.

- Overhaul the landscaping and keep the gardener mowing while he waited for payment from Europe.

Then I could sell the property. Or hope to, because, as you know, that's all subject to finding a willing buyer, the lender's mood, and the phase of the moon. But I'm not complaining.[15]

---

15   This one closed. I got paid.

All that labor looked like a picnic compared to working with Big Bad Bank, the holder of the mortgage on the property. Here's how that went down:

December

13: I receive my Christmas gift from the Universe: the seller's daughter signs the listing. I tell Big Bad Bank that I am in possession of the listing, I am ~~dreading~~ overjoyed to be working with them, and how can I satisfy their every need?

15: I tell them again.

17-31: I tell them again and again and again.

January

5: Big Bad Bank responds—"A ~~robot~~ negotiator will be assigned to this case."
I wait. And I wait. I call. I wait. And I wait.

I am unable to get onto The Platter to perform this task, so I call their main number:

Me: "I think I need a password."

Big Bad Bank: "Your negotiator will give that to you."

Me: "May I please have his phone number?"

Big Bad Bank: "No. All communication must be done on The Platter."

Me: "I can't get there from here."

Big Bad Bank: "Harold will contact you."

Meanwhile, we get into contract with a buyer who should have known better, but she'd heard that short sales are a good deal. They would be if the bank weren't involved.

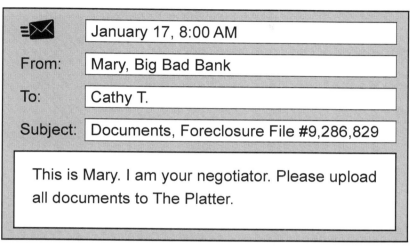

January 17, 8:00 AM

From: Mary, Big Bad Bank

To: Cathy T.

Subject: Documents, Foreclosure File #9,286,829

This is Mary. I am your negotiator. Please upload all documents to The Platter.

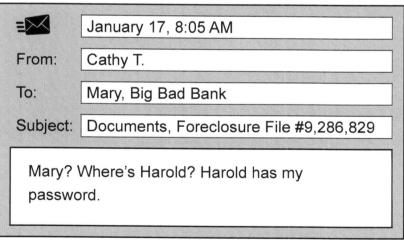

January 17, 8:05 AM

From: Cathy T.

To: Mary, Big Bad Bank

Subject: Documents, Foreclosure File #9,286,829

Mary? Where's Harold? Harold has my password.

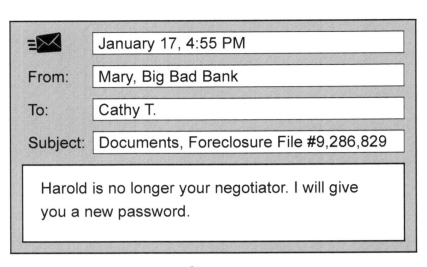

January 17, 4:55 PM

From: Mary, Big Bad Bank

To: Cathy T.

Subject: Documents, Foreclosure File #9,286,829

Harold is no longer your negotiator. I will give you a new password.

18: I receive my password!

I log on and learn that every ~~demand~~ request that Big Bad Bank makes on The Platter has a color code—green means submit today (today being defined as 5 p.m. in whatever time zone the negotiator is based or is thinking of vacationing in); yellow means noon today; orange means "Now!"; and red means "You are screwed."

I think Mary wants to get off on the right foot because she gives me a green light to upload the documents, of which there are 900 pages. The Platter callously rejects my effort. I try again. It jubilantly rejects me (how would *you* interpret "Ha, ha!"?). The third time, with the 5 p.m. deadline approaching, I frantically call the bank's main number which prompts an auto-response e-mail from Mary:

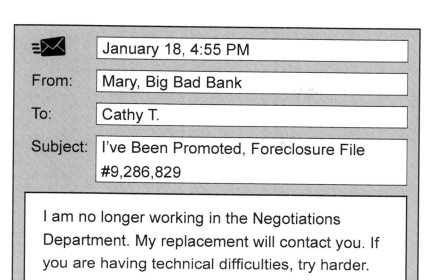

January 18, 4:55 PM

From: Mary, Big Bad Bank

To: Cathy T.

Subject: I've Been Promoted, Foreclosure File #9,286,829

I am no longer working in the Negotiations Department. My replacement will contact you. If you are having technical difficulties, try harder.

I don't panic, though. What's there to lose? *A buyer?!*

≡✉	January 20, 8:05 AM
From:	Charles, Big Bad Bank
To:	Cathy T.
Subject:	Mary Doesn't Work Here Anymore, Foreclosure File #9,286,829

This is Charles. I am your negotiator. I see that you have had access to The Platter since January 5, and have not complied with our instructions. This is a warning. Your offer will not be considered, and your relationship with Big Bad Bank will be severed permanently, if you do not upload the required documentation immediately. By the way, we started foreclosure proceedings.

Oh. Guess my client reneged on her promise to keep paying the mortgage.

From: Cathy T.

To: Charles, Big Bad Bank

Subject: Mary Doesn't Work Here Anymore, Foreclosure File #9,286,829

Listen, Charles, we need to talk. I mean ear-to-ear. What does the bank charge for your phone number?

Mother of God! Charles calls me—from an unidentified phone, probably in the bank's cafeteria. And I succeed in uploading my documents.

February

≡✉   February 1, 8:05 AM

From: Jennifer, Big Bad Bank

To: Cathy T.

Subject: Charles Doesn't Work Here Anymore,
              Foreclosure File #9,286,829

> This is Jennifer. I am your negotiator. Please
> upload all pertinent documentation to The
> Platter.

Jennifer? I'd been *wondering* where Charles
was. And what he was doing with my documents.
I send an orange e-mail to The Platter Technical
Support. Fortuitously, I had come across their phone
number while ~~hacking into~~ researching the number
for the bank's president, so I also call:

Me: "Just wondering what happened to all the
documentation I uploaded and for which I have a
dated acknowledgement."

I wait. And I wait. They're playing nice music
on the hold line, which reminds me of a concert I
had attended over the holidays, and the wristwatch I

did not get for Christmas. My daydream is abruptly terminated by a voice at the other end of the line stating that:

"We are too busy to talk to you. Your call will be returned in twenty-four hours." Click.

2: It's very important to keep the other agent informed along the way. At twenty-four hours plus one, I call the other agent:

Me: "I contacted Big Bad Bank today and reminded them that we are into the second twenty-four-hour callback period. I'll check again later."

At twenty-four hours plus two, I call Big Bad Bank and actually talk into a live ear. I am put on hold while its mouth says they would try to locate whoever is my negotiator that day.

≡✉	February 2, 1:30 PM
From:	Cathy T.
To:	BobTheBuyer'sAgent
Subject:	You'd Want to Know, 2689 Maple St.

It is now 1:30 p.m. and I have heard a complete Mahler symphony on hold. I think they're reviewing our file. I don't know. This is very stressful. I found a watch online that I can't afford to buy, especially if this escrow doesn't close. By the way, they started to foreclose.

At 4:55 p.m. I hang up on the bank and call back. They are still playing Mahler. Someone picks up the phone and hangs up again.

3: Next morning: I log on.

The Platter has a message for me!

"Big Bad Bank has reactivated your file." *Reactivated?* "We will notify you regarding the approval or disapproval of the purchase offer in two weeks. Don't forget we're foreclosing!"

I am invested in this transaction—they've got 900 pieces of paper that I, personally, uploaded. And I want that watch. I *deserve* that watch. But that aside,

I must save my client's credit rating and help her do the right thing. Which is wallow in the mud with Big Bad Bank until we get this short sale closed versus tossing in the towel and just letting them sit on their nonperforming asset until *they* can sell it.

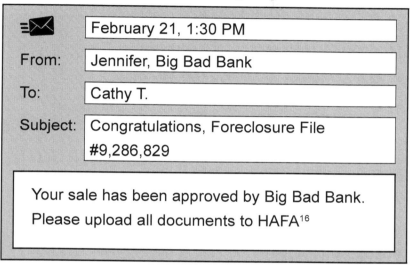

✉	February 21, 1:30 PM
From:	Jennifer, Big Bad Bank
To:	Cathy T.
Subject:	Congratulations, Foreclosure File #9,286,829

Your sale has been approved by Big Bad Bank. Please upload all documents to HAFA[16]

Harold and Mary and Charles forgot to tell me HAFA was involved, and they hadn't copied them on all the documents. Jennifer didn't feel like doing it herself because "Harold or Mary or Charles should have taken care of that." By this point, the bank has brought the total page count up to 1,000.

---

16   Multiple choice: HAFA is defined as (A) Home Affordable Foreclosure Alternatives; (B) Hmong American Friendship Association; (C) Houston Area Ferret Association.

From: Cathy T.

To: BobTheBuyer'sAgent

Subject: The Roller Coaster Is Back in Operation, 2689 Maple St.

Hi, BobTheBuyer'sAgent,

And you didn't know it was off the tracks! So glad I could spare you. The other news is that we now have another 2.5-week wait after I upload every single piece of paper that Big Bad Bank already has to HAFA, which I will do with the utmost gratitude for their rescuing our transaction from the brink of annihilation. I never thought I'd be so happy to perform redundant tasks repeatedly.

As you know, they're foreclosing. But I've been assured a postponement is "no sweat."

March

13: Why am I not surprised that I don't have a decision back from HAFA? I call Jennifer and conference in the buyer's agent so that he hears the distress in my voice. Jennifer informs us that three days earlier, HAFA had reviewed the file and requested more clarification from Big Bad Bank, so "thanks for reminding me to look at the file."

My client calls, *calls*, from Europe, "just wondering" how things are going. I tell her. She's really very nice. She observes that reporting on these marvels of corporate efficiency is how Scott Adams made millions of dollars.

I need to shop for a less expensive watch.

✉	March 25, 1:35 PM
From:	Jennifer, Big Bad Bank
To:	Cathy T.
Subject:	Congratulations, Foreclosure File #9,286,829
Attach:	The Attachment

HAFA and Big Bad Bank have reviewed all 900 pages of documentation that you uploaded. There should have been 1,000. Here is what we need to move forward: see attachment.

Attachment:

1. An updated proof of funds with buyer's maternal grandfather's DNA on the statement.

2. An updated hardship letter with greater detail on the seller's suffering. We enjoy reading those. Photos would be good, too.

3. A HUD statement printed on 24 lb., 25% recycled rag bond, with wet signatures, more recent than the one that escrow prepared yesterday.

4. The remaining items listed on pages 1-50 of The Attachment.

March 26, 4:00 PM

From: Cathy T.

To: Jennifer, Big Bad Bank

Subject: Your Request, Foreclosure File #9,286,829

Attach: Attachments 1-50

Jennifer,

I have everything you requested and have tried, unsuccessfully, to upload these documents to The Platter all day. This may have something to do with The Platter not recognizing my computer because I am doing this remotely, from the Costco Business Center ~~while I shop for my watch~~.

Jennifer, we have an agreed upon sale price and an ALL CASH buyer. Your bank is losing ~~its asset~~ money on this asset every day, and you aren't getting the paperwork because The Platter is lousy software and the support is even worse!

CAN'T YOU DO SOMETHING ABOUT THIS?

Warmest wishes, Cathy

April

I hear nothing from Big Bad Bank during the month of April. They are either giving me a time-out for my insolence or their calendar has eleven months. But I was busily working behind the scenes.

May

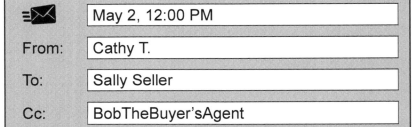

May 2, 12:00 PM

From: Cathy T.

To: Sally Seller

Cc: BobTheBuyer'sAgent

Subject: Update, Mom's House, 2689 Maple St.

Happy Friday! We just did an end-run around Big Bad Bank, thanks to my new BFF. His name is Mort and he lives at HAFA. He just let me e-mail him all the documents that The Platter wouldn't accept.

This is very good news because it means that your agent will not be fined or imprisoned and can continue to work on your behalf to get this escrow closed before Big Bad Bank forecloses.

May 2, 2:00 PM
From:	Sally Seller
To:	Cathy T.
Subject:	Update, Mom's House, 2689 Maple St.

Thanks for the update. My coworker told me that 70 percent of all short sales end up going to foreclosure. We wonder why banks continue to walk past offers and take less money in foreclosure.

May 2, 2:05 PM.
From:	Cathy T.
To:	Sally Seller
Subject:	Update, Mom's House, 2689 Maple St.

Because the inmates are running the asylum.

XO, Cathy

6: Speaking of foreclosure, it's about time to ask for an extension, which I had been told was, you know, "no sweat." It is now Foreclosure Sale

Day (May 20) minus 14, and if history is any
indication...

≡✉	May 6, 8:00 AM
From:	Cathy T.
To:	Jennifer, Big Bad Bank
Subject:	Foreclosure - Foreclosure File #9,286,829

Hi, Jennifer,

I know you're still waiting to hear from HAFA, but
can we get that extension? Just in case?

≡✉	May 10, 4:55 PM
From:	Jennifer, Big Bad Bank
To:	Cathy T.
Subject:	Foreclosure - Foreclosure File #9,286,829

I don't think we'll need it.

The countdown begins. 10, 9, 8, 7 days...

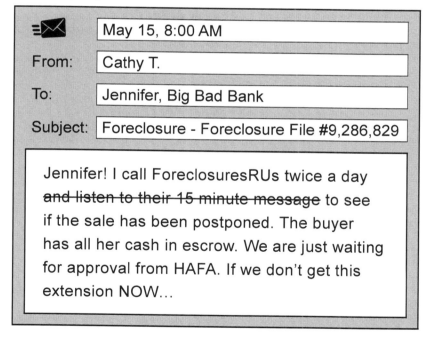

May 13, 8:00 AM

From: Cathy T.

To: Jennifer, Big Bad Bank

Subject: Foreclosure - Foreclosure File #9,286,829

We need a postponement.

6, 5 days...

May 15, 8:00 AM

From: Cathy T.

To: Jennifer, Big Bad Bank

Subject: Foreclosure - Foreclosure File #9,286,829

Jennifer! I call ForeclosuresRUs twice a day
~~and listen to their 15-minute message~~ to see
if the sale has been postponed. The buyer
has all her cash in escrow. We are just waiting
for approval from HAFA. If we don't get this
extension NOW...

	May 15, 12:00 PM
From:	Cathy T.
To:	Sally Seller
Cc:	BobTheBuyer'sAgent
Subject:	Update, 2689 Maple St.

Hello, troops,

Mort is no longer my BFF, and BBB is engaged in a game of chicken with us. I fear I may have to reprise my role as loud, obnoxious advocate for the little guy against Big Bad Bank at the courthouse steps—a performance that was hailed with high-fives last year when I took the family with three autistic kids to stop Worst Bank at the courthouse. It worked. You're in good hands. I'll use the same signs. What's a little poetic license?

	May 18, 4:55 PM
From:	Jennifer, Big Bad Bank
To:	Cathy T.
Subject:	Foreclosure - Foreclosure File #9,286,829

Oh, we don't put in for those until two days before the sale.

	May 18, 4:57 PM.
From:	Cathy T.
To:	Jennifer, Big Bad Bank
Subject:	Foreclosure - Foreclosure File #9,286,829

Jennifer, that would be today!

	May 19, Noon
From:	Cathy T.
To:	Sally Seller, BobTheBuyer'sAgent
Subject:	Update, 2689 Maple St.

As you know, we are scheduled to go to sale tomorrow at 1:30 PM. This is not the sale we want. Jennifer tells me she has put in twice for a postponement with the assistant to the manager of the department that puts in for postponements through the Secretary to the Director of the Office of Postponements. I asked if she talked to a live person. She said she didn't know.

Meanwhile, I call ForeclosuresRUs three times a day to see if our sale date got moved. In between those calls, I send e-mails and call HAFA to remind them to look at our file.

I call BobTheBuyer's Agent: "I know your purchase contract was written with a 45-day close. ~~PLEEEEASE~~ Please let me know that your client ~~hasn't given up~~ will be ready to close as soon as we get final approval."

God, I need that watch.

At 10 a.m. on May 20, ForeclosuresRUs informs me that the sale has been postponed for two months.

And then:

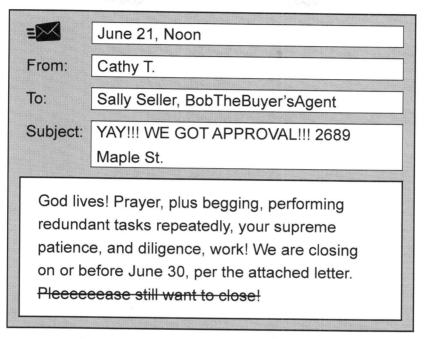

June 21, Noon

From: Cathy T.

To: Sally Seller, BobTheBuyer'sAgent

Subject: YAY!!! WE GOT APPROVAL!!! 2689 Maple St.

God lives! Prayer, plus begging, performing redundant tasks repeatedly, your supreme patience, and diligence, work! We are closing on or before June 30, per the attached letter. ~~Pleeeeeease still want to close!~~

And close we did—on July 10. Somehow, though, it seemed anticlimactic. But my new watch is awesome.

"*Energy and persistence conquer all things.*"

Benjamin Franklin

Chapter 16

Foreclosures: Nearer My God to Thee

That's how I learned never to do a short sale again. If given a choice between doing a short sale and not eating, I would not eat. Foreclosures are a close second. Yes, I had to curb my appetite during the mortgage crisis, but I can wear my tightest pants now.

The problem with foreclosures is that you have little control. And that's if you're the listing agent. If you represent the buyer, well, imagine yourself...no, don't. It's like childbirth. If you knew, you wouldn't have babies and then there'd be no Realtors to sell houses to innocent young families who get loans from big bad banks who (how did this happen?) came out smelling as fresh as new money after the housing crisis; it would be the end of civilization as we know it. So just don't think about it.

One cold, rainy, windy, terrible November (Thanksgiving to be precise) the daughter and son-in-law of my surrogate sister decided it was The Perfect Time to buy their first home. And they would "help" me, to make it easier, because after all it was the holiday season, and "You shouldn't have to work now."

"How 'bout we wait until after Christmas; there'll be lots more foreclosures on the market then," I selflessly suggested.

"Sure, but we'll just start doing some research on our own," they sweetly replied.

Divine intervention—we found the house in less than a month. On December 17. The house was gorgeous; why was it still here after thirty days on the market per the kids, who had found it on some real estate service in the sky? Why couldn't I find it on *my* Multiple Listing Service? Why was there no "For Sale" sign out front? It became evident very soon: this house was not on the listing agent's radar.

Have you noticed that some foreclosure agents become quite impressed with themselves? That their heads swell in proportion to the number of listings they have? This fellow had over 200 listings; he was waaaay beyond big headed—he had become...a deity! When you are this huge, you're much too important to talk to the buyer's agent. You delegate. And use e-mail when there's no avoiding the other agent.

God's assistant, Thor, who did all God's bidding and to whom I was relegated, was most charming—while he was here. On December 21 he announced to me that he would be on vacation until "after Christmas." So for that week, during which we had to have all of our inspections and remove all of our contingencies to meet the foreclosure lender's deadline, Thor would be gone. Oh well, he could put together whatever fell apart on the following Monday. He also promised me seller's signatures on the purchase contract the next day, as he cheerily signed off.

On December 23 we were scheduled for a home inspection, a pest inspection, a fireplace inspection, and a roof inspection—so fortunate to get any inspectors out during Christmas week, and luckier still that they agreed to be there on the same day. To be on the safe side we went to the house to assure that the water and power were on, as we had been told. Power—yes. Water—no.

I call Thor's office:

Me: "Water's not on."

Secretary: "Yes it is."

Me: "Really, well it's not coming out of the pipes."

Secretary: "I'll call the water department and call you back."

Four hours later (two days before Inspection Day) I call Thor's office:

Me: "Any answer on the water?"

Secretary: "They haven't called me back."

How proactive. I refrain from commenting and, instead, call the water department myself:

Me: "I'm told the water is supposed to be on at that cute little foreclosure house."

Water department: "No, God hasn't paid the back water bill."

I call God's secretary:

Me: "You have to pay the bill before they'll turn the water on."

Secretary: "Oh. I can't do that."

Me: "Really, well who can?" Sugar would melt in my mouth.

Secretary: "God."

Me: "Well, may I please speak to God?"

Secretary: "He's in a meeting; you can leave a voice mail."

I call God's voice mail and get his "I'm such a mellow guy if you're a lender calling to give me another foreclosure listing" voice. I leave my message.

The next morning (one day before the four inspections) I get a call from the secretary:

"God took care of it."

Being on the cautious side, I call the water department.

"No, we haven't heard from Him."

I call God's office again and share this feedback. Only this time I'm getting tired, and scared. The secretary says, "Call God's wife."

I leave a message for her, explaining our urgency. God's wife (who you can be sure had better things to do with all his money at Christmastime than deal with us) was MIA. At 4 p.m. she calls me:

Mrs. God: IT'S TAKEN CARE OF!

Me: OK! Thank you! Merry Christmas!

I go to the house. The...water...is...not...on.

At this point, I have no choice. I *must* talk to God! I leave Him a voice mail, words to the effect of: I am so unworthy, but please, merciful God, have pity on these lowly first-time homebuyers who need shelter. *I must have an audience with you!*

God returns my phone call! He sure has a different voice in person. In his Other Agent Voice he imperiously informs me that he has "220 foreclosure listings and this is just a little water bill," and "Don't question ME!" At the risk of committing a mortal sin, I do question him enough that it sounds like he actually might have a doubt himself. So I am ordered to call the water department again and report back to Him.

I call the water department and get the manager, who actually looks at the right computer screen and says, "They paid the water bill." Hallelujah. Now it's just a (relatively simple) matter of getting the field guy out there the next morning, the day before Christmas Eve, before noon, to remove the lock on the water meter so we can proceed with our four inspections. Which did happen. Which is not the end of this story.

True to his word, Thor returns "after Christmas"... on January 4. Now we'd like to close escrow. But the signed purchase contract that he had promised me two weeks before had still not materialized. You see, with foreclosures the buyer (and his agent) spend hours and hours and hundreds of dollars trusting that the foreclosure lender will honor his verbal commitment and actually *sign* the contract. This, of course, increases the buyer's anxiety and his agent's urge to kill. Lenders abide by the Golden Rule: We have the gold, so we make the rules.

I call Thor and say, "Happy New Year, we've been in escrow eighteen days, have fulfilled all terms, our lender is ready to close, and we just need a signed contract." No response.

I try again. No response.

I call God. No response.

My buyers call me.

"When are we going to close?"

Me: "WHEN GOD SAYS SO! Sorry, kids, it must be getting to me. But seriously, you'll know as soon as I do because the skies will part, winged angels will appear, trumpets will blow, and your signed purchase contract will drop from the sky."

After seven more days of monitoring the heavens, I received the signed purchase contract and we closed escrow.

I would say this account should go into the annals of real estate sales, but it's just the way it is.

Waxing poetic:
Foreclosures are a niche
that rhymes with...

Chapter 17

Of Course I Do Rentals! Useful Rhetoric

"Eeeeeew," you say.

Let's not be negative, here. There are reasons why you *would* want to lease property:

1. You like to debate.

2. You have masochistic tendencies.

3. You're lonely and like all the phone calls.

4. You *really* need the money.

5. Penance.

Besides, you sold your client the property and he expects you to help him. Here is the dichotomy: you know tenants are living, breathing, sentient beings; the landlord sees them as ATMs.

Unlike a sale, where the buyers close escrow and live happily ever after, tenants and their landlords become your extended family. They remember you at Christmas:

Landlord: "The tenant says the toilet backed up and flooded the downstairs. I'm out of town. Can you handle it?"

They know when you're leaving on vacation:

Tenant: "We bought a house. We're moving."

Landlord: "I need the money; can you put it on the market *now*?"

Even if you don't manage the property after leasing it, they still call you.[17] And they call each other, forever— the tenant wanting the landlord to fix things, to make improvements, to be patient about late rent payments and bouncy checks; the landlord conferencing you into the call to explain to the tenant what it said in the lease he signed.

It's important that we agents do a better job of leasing the property than the landlord himself could, or how else can we justify the $1.10 per hour we earn? In many ways it's more labor-intensive than a sale. We:

1. Show the property ourselves. Other agents can't be bothered.

2. Screen the calls for more than just the ability to pay, carefully avoiding questions that could

---

17   Shout-out to clients: It's okay—keep those calls comin' ☺.

smack of discrimination.

3. Wrack our brains for courteous responses to "we're leaving our husbands, and we want to rent your house." Or, "I'm pregnant; it just 'happened.' No, I don't have a job, get alimony, or child support...maybe I should just meet the landlord."

4. Write the lease. Which, with addenda, is longer than a purchase contract.

5. Make sure the landlord fills out the Move-In, Move-Out form. Pester him repeatedly, for weeks after the tenant occupies. Remind him that it's for his own good. Smile when he says, "Can't you do it for me?"

6. On the off chance that there's a different agent for the tenant, work diligently to extricate the MIMO from him.

I don't want to repeat this exercise often. So, when a landlord tells me what a big pain in the neck it is ~~to do it the right way~~ to rent a place out, I say, "Right. Let's find you a forever tenant!"

Jonah and Faith were, indeed, forever tenant material. They loved the house after they chased the rats out, mowed down the waist-high weeds, and disinfected every accessible surface. They loved it because it meant their kids would be in a better school district, and there was room to move Faith's mom out from Florida where she gave up a good job to take care of her grandchildren. They loved it because their previous landlord, who had assured them that he would never sell the house out from under them, did just that twelve months after they moved in. But that was not going to happen here, because these landlords wanted *forever* tenants.

Well, over the next year during which Jonah and Faith made so many improvements and fixed the house up so cute, the real estate market turned around and the home rose to the "above water" mark for the first time in five years. Oooh, bad timing. That wasn't supposed to happen. And the home that the owners said they'd "never, ever, sell because we need to stay invested," went on the market. The heartbreak of capitalism.

Occasionally, I do get a landlord with heart. Too much heart. Which requires me to put on my wolf hat and become the bad guy, because it's a Realtor's fiduciary duty to protect the client from himself...or herself...or the spouse.

Herb did the legwork for the family's rentals. Mathilda did the books. Herb loved to putter around at the homes and was often there when prospective tenants drove up. He was an incorrigible people-pleaser, which became a problem when I tried to reconcile what he told renters with what was written in the listing.

Everything was moving along swimmingly. Herb and the prospective tenant had met. Her credit and employment checked out. Time to draw up the lease.

Me: "Janie is so excited! She gave notice where she lives and wants to occupy as soon as we get this lease signed. We'll just write in that the new washer and dryer will be delivered after she moves in, and that the concrete company will install the patio when the weather improves."

Mathilda: "What new washer and dryer?"

Herb: Silence.

Mathilda: "What patio? Where'd she get those ideas?"

I look at Herb. Herb is not looking at me.

Me: "Don't worry about it." *I will.*

And then there's the Dutiful Daughter. The one who wants to reserve all options for her mom:

Me: "So, you'd rather do a month-to-month than a year's lease? You know that will make it easier for the tenant to leave."

Dutiful Daughter: "But what if my mom wants to move back into the house in a few months? She might not like the rest home." Well, I'm glad we had that chat.

Professional property managers deal with this stuff every day. They have nerves of steel, the patience of Job, and the ability to administer tough love. Not me. So I've developed some handy rhetoric for escaping property management: "Why would you want to pay me over a hundred dollars a month (always use numbers) to collect the rent and occasionally call a repairman when you can easily do that yourself? I'll give you contractor contacts when you need them. There, you just saved yourself a lot of money."

If that doesn't do the trick, I refer them to a professional property management company that I know won't steal the listing if the owner decides to sell. Regardless, it's worth the risk.

Ask yourself: Am I constitutionally suited to leasing?

Chapter 18

Farming: The Absolute Best Tool for Success– A Primer

"Cathy, Cathy, Cathy. I don't know why you waste your time with those little houses," remarked a Realtor acquaintance of mine one day. He was referring to my middle-income farm as compared to the executive mansions he sold as a relocation agent.

All Samuel had to do was wine and dine his corporate contacts and then shake the tree for listings.

"Well, Samuel, I live in one of those little houses. I have nice neighbors. Their homes sell five times more often than the executive mansions you sell. Do the math."

And when the economy turned and companies lightened up on executives, executive transfers, and relocation agents, there went his business. Same thing happened to my friend the foreclosure agent when his three sources ran dry. A well-tended farm would have saved their bacon.

Farming is work. But, as I said before, what else are you going to do while you aren't selling houses? I farmed. I busied myself writing a monthly newsletter. It was 11 x 17, folded in half, with print on both sides. I spent hours culling real estate news, composing helpful articles, analyzing sales statistics, and gathering ads for residents with things to sell or services to offer. I also included stories about my "poodle from hell" and our deaf Dalmatian, to show that I'm human. The dogs had a hilarious dynamic going, and I was their foil.

I slaved over that newsletter, and residents told me their favorite parts were the dog stories and the statistics. The message here is that you don't have to work as hard as I did. Yours can be just one 8.5 x 11 page. There are so many services today that provide downloadable articles to use, and your local board or state Realtor association probably does a pretty neat, camera-ready template. Check out ActiveRain.com—the largest real estate-oriented group on the web—and you'll get marvelous ideas from their blog and services.

If you want to be warm and fuzzy, share a couple paragraphs about a silly thing that happened to you, or a nice congratulations to a resident. Keep It Simple Smartie. There are so many things you can write very short articles about: inexpensive improvements to the home that return more than their cost; how prices in your market area compare to others in the region; renting versus buying. Add a client testimonial to boost your authority, and always mention that they can call you for referrals to good contractors (whom you've checked out with the Contractors State Licensing Board).

Consistency is all-important; don't give up if it doesn't produce immediate results. It will. Your competition will wear out. I repeat: What else would you be doing while you wait for a listing or a buyer?

As for distribution, it's important that your farm sees you sweat, out walking your newsletter. Maybe not every month, but enough that they recognize you when they do see you. For months when you are too busy to walk it, avail yourself of the easy alternative to the torture of Bulk Mail: the Post Office's Every Door Direct Mail service, EDDM. It's simple, cheap, and fast. You don't even need mailing labels! Just print your marketing piece following the Post Office's guidelines. Then go online, define the map boundaries for distribution, print out the cover sheets, bundle the articles into stacks, and deliver to the post office. If I can do this, you can, and I could not handle Bulk Mail by myself.

Do not worry that your newsletter isn't all slick and glossy like something General Motors would send. Homeowners are much more likely to read a piece that you obviously created. And it's so much easier to put together your own newsletter now than it was twenty-five years ago.

You'll want to make a splash in your farm with activities. One of my early service projects was Santa for the Kids. I bought a beautiful red velvet Santa suit and found a volunteer to put into it. I leased the Elks Club for an afternoon and announced free candy canes, a session with Santa, and photos, compliments of me and my real estate company. The first year I had 100 kids; the second year, about twenty-five. The parents probably remembered that I couldn't work the camera well and got their photos mixed up. I've repressed the details.

Next and forever after, I held annual garage sales. When my archrival observed that they attracted a lot of attention (125 homes at one point), he decided to participate, too—by holding one on exactly the same day as mine. He continued doing that for a couple of years, until I thwarted him by not having one. He stopped holding them after that, and then I resumed.

You know how to do a garage sale. It's in your blood. So just a few tips:

- Notify the farm of the garage sale date two months in advance. Any further out and most will forget or lose the flyer.

- One month before, send them entry forms asking them to list a few items for sale so you can draw buyers to their home.

- Type up the list and use a GPS program to locate each address on the map that you'll put on the back side of the list. This will earn you rave reviews.

- On garage sale day, do not visit the homes— they'll think you're stalking them. Sit at the entry to the neighborhood with your lists, smile, and wave at everyone who goes by. They know why you do garage sales.

- If you have a dog, bring him. His enthusiasm won't wane after five hours sitting at the corner watching cars go by.

The point of this exercise is not to get listings—it's to infiltrate the public's subconscious so that when they think of real estate they think of you. Whatever you do, don't amble up someone's driveway to deliver doughnuts and ask if they're getting rid of all their stuff because they're moving. I have actually seen homeowners recoil into the back of their garage when thusly approached. By another agent.

When you farm, your reputation precedes you. Word gets around quickly if you don't treat people right. Always, always, always put their best interests ahead of your own. We're Realtors. It's assumed that we're in this for the money, so people are always suspicious of our motives. Here is some verbiage that got me listings and kept my clients happy:

- I won't represent the buyer if I list your home.

- Here's where the market is and where I believe your home should be priced. We'll ask anything you want, and I'll defend it like it's my idea, but I want to go on record as telling you where I believe your home should be priced so you don't get mad at me if we don't get what you're asking.

- Let's get a second or third bid for repairs.

- I'll take a half-percent off of my commission; I want you to feel that I'm doing everything I can to help you.

It's pretty simple. People want to know that you're on their side, and they can tell when you're taking the easy way out. They talk. Like at open houses when a neighbor comes in to vent about how she got totally taken by her agent. Her rapt audience hangs on every word. Do everything you can to let your clients know how important they are to you.

Living in your farm can bolster your career. The downside, however, is that you are too available. I've been mistaken for a sitting duck on several occasions. Like when the neighbor knocked on my door with an adorable black miniature poodle in her arms:

"Hi! My son just got a hunting dog, and said the poodle has to go. Can you put an ad in your newsletter?"

Me: "Of course! I'll be delighted to help you find a home for her."

Mrs. Mom: "Oh, good. And will you keep her until then? Here," she said, shoving Mimi into my arms.

And if you can't park your car in the garage because your husband's sports car lives there, you must always be dressed for success so residents don't think you're goofing off when you're at home. Don't ever garden on a weekday. Shop for groceries after dark. The benefits of farming definitely outweigh the drawbacks, though. For instance, you have a built-in spy network. Priceless. An occupational hazard in real estate is all those people who call us out to share the benefit of our years of experience, to advise them on fix-ups, to appraise their home—people who have no intention whatsoever of listing with us;

they're going to list with their friend. If you offered to sell their house for free, they'd just go back to the friend and ask her to match or beat your offer.

I'm not talking about the "we want to interview three Realtors" people, who honestly don't know which agent to choose. Competition is part of our MO and we have to deal with it. I'm talking about cold, hard, calculated, wasters of our time.

You may be saying to yourself, "Well, if I have to give away my time to compete anyway, what difference does it make?" The answer is: You have a chance with the three-interview people; it's a hedged bet. We're risk-takers, not doormats.

Mr. and Mrs. Melody called me out one spring day to discuss the eventual sale of their home in my farm. Daughter Annie had been raised in that home and still lived in the neighborhood. I thought it strange that not once during the two hours I spent with them, going through the house, giving them recommendations for fix-ups, discussing comparable sales, and arriving at an opinion of value, did she smile or say a word. My radar went up.

A month later I got a call from the Melodys' son who made a special trip to California to "talk about putting Mom's and Dad's home on the market and determine the asking price." Luckily for me, though, I had just sold a home that belonged to Annie's friend—a friend who, knowing nothing about my involvement with the Melodys, told me that Annie's parents were going to sell their home, and she would have referred me but knew they were going to list with Annie's Realtor friend. So when the son called I was too busy to give away any more of my time.

Another occupational hazard is poachers. The more listings you get in an area, the more visible you become to other agents looking for fertile farm land. You make it look so easy. You just send out a newsletter, have a garage sale, and, *voilá!* They list with you. So it did not surprise me one day as I sat at my kitchen table sharing a tuna fish sandwich with my poodle to see Ninja Nancy in her blue jeans and tennies bouncing from door to door. She landed on my porch and before she could utter, "Oh! You live here," she had thrust a flyer at me.

"How are you, Nancy?" I asked.

"I'm doing great. I'm farming your neighborhood."

"Well, there's always room for one more," I said. "Competition brings out the best in us, huh?"

Ninja Nancy lasted about eight months.

Then Rosey and Ronald, two agents who lived in my neighborhood, figured that if I had had such luck doing garage sales, they would clinch a takeover by holding a garage sale and a barbecue on Ronald's driveway. Their plan, in the words of my spy, was to "take over Cathy's farm."

All of these agents were doing the right thing—they were trying to build their business by farming. And they probably could have succeeded had they stuck it out, because no one agent can be everything to everyone. The secret to taking over a farm is perseverance.

It's worth it. Farming has gotten me named in people's wills; my spy network saved me from listing a home whose owner had painted over rampant mold; they let me know that my client's daughter whom I hired to pass out my newsletters dumped the whole bunch in the trash. I can't stress strongly enough the value of farming.

So when another agent asks why I bother with farming, I just say my livelihood depends on it.

Farm!

Chapter 19

Technology and Social Media (S&M)

How did Realtors get anything done before technology happened? Now we can update our business portraits with Photoshop and work at home in our pajamas. And cell phones filter sound so well that we can even walk the dogs while negotiating a contract.

But technology has a dark side: somebody has to figure it out and keep it working. My solution was to marry an engineer. He solves all my technology problems by researching and buying me a new whatever it is that he bought me a while back but there's a slicker model out now.

I have five software programs to get the house photos out of my camera, into my computer, and onto a brochure. This is not good because I have not mastered any of them. Next month there may be a sixth. For my birthday MyHusbandTheEngineer bought me a new camera. I needed it like I needed the fourth TV set he got me for Christmas in response to my constant complaint that I wish I had a TV I could operate.

"Oh, thank you, sweetheart," I smiled. "Now how is this camera an improvement on the ones I already have?" Which are pink, which this one is not, which is the first rule for buying me anything with movable parts—it must be pink because that makes it less intimidating.

"You need this for real estate." His rationalization for spending hours at his favorite hobby, research. Then he handed the manual to me and remembered he had an appointment.

That part of our marriage doesn't always work well. Fortunately, the Board of Realtors provides couples counseling...aka, Technical Support.

"Hi! Help!" I don't even need to give them my name anymore.

"What's your browser, again?" Christopher asks.

"How do I tell that?"

"Never mind. Would you object to my taking control of your computer with Bomgar?"

"Would you?! Please...I can't do anything with it."

"What's your password?"

Me: "IHATETHISWEBSITE, all caps."

Christopher: "And what is the problem today?"

Me: "I can't find the pictures I took."

Christopher: "Where did you put them?"

Me: "Christopher, you're starting to sound like my husband. Now, if I knew, why would I be calling you?"

I love Christopher. I don't have to cry or threaten to withhold dinner and he fixes my pictures.

As if photos were not a big enough challenge, I had to upgrade to an iPhone because my ~~Rasp~~Blackberry wouldn't do e-mail. I am a PC person. This was a paradigm shift. I took MyHusbandTheEngineer with me to the Apple store to interpret, to bridge the gap between my concept of the problem and what the techie would ask.

I presented my fuchsia-colored phone and pile of yellow stickies to the techie, and my husband said, "She wants to practice FaceTime with the dogs, before she tries it on clients."

The techie: "Oh very simple. You just hit this button to get the main screen up, then touch the fifth button on the third screen you get to after you rhinoceros the washing machine. If you fruitcake the taco you'll get to France which is where you kangaroo the Twinkie. Follow?"

"Of course," I answered. "It's so transparent. I also don't know how to text."

"Oh, simpleton!" he exclaimed. "Let's just pull up that screen...MY GAWD! You have 20,000 text messages here—unopened! What plan are you on?"

"The one with supplemental psychiatric care. I distinctly remember signing up for that."

"Well, let's see. Do you have any friends—or family?"

"None who are technologically inclined, present company excluded."

"Good. Because the new plan forbids friends and especially family. But you can reduce your monthly bill 30 percent by choosing to forsake any real social activity you might have been participating in."

"Did you say 30 percent off?!" I asked.

"Yes. But then your friends and family will disappear."

"Where will they go?"

"Well, into our database, of course. But they won't even miss you—we'll be more in touch with them than you ever were."

"For 30 percent less. Hmmmm...Can you close the messages with 'XO, Cathy'?"

"Personal messages reduce the reduction to 25 percent."

I ponder this. It's clear to me that one can either operate technological devices or do meaningful work; you can't have it both ways. So, I think getting a sizable discount on my bill and letting the rhinoceroses and kangaroos maintain my social life, thereby freeing me to sell real estate, is a fair trade. Yes! Technology working for me!

Find yourself a techie and never let him go.

Chapter 20

You Want Me to Sell *This*?

What are the most memorable homes you've ever seen or sold? Some of my sales stay with me like PTSD. Surprise attacks. Out of the blue. One day you're thinking everyone lives like you, the next minute, *Wham!* You never know what you'll find when you're invited to someone's home.

Mr. Hunter: "I'd like you to come over and talk to me about selling our ~~museum~~ house. We live at 4321 Aardvark Street."

Me: "Great. Know the neighborhood well. Tell me about your home."

Mr. Hunter: "It's 2,600 square feet, and we've completely remodeled: kitchen, baths, windows, everything. And it's already staged for you."

Don't you love it when you know exactly what you'll see before you get there? You have your presentation memorized. You could do this in your sleep.

I drove up to the picture-perfect house. Mrs. Hunter opened the door and waved me in.

Oh. My. God. Smokey the Bear stared me in the eye. To his right, Bambi. I was ushered into the family room and seated next to Old Yeller. I was speechless.

Mrs. Hunter offered me coffee.

"Do you have anything stronger?" I wanted to ask. I declined.

Mr. Hunter joined us and explained that they needed to acquire a larger home for their collection, and then informed me that (you can't improve on perfection) the home was ready to show:

"The animals stay, but we'll remove the guns."

I could hardly gasp. If I opened my mouth, I'd sob. I might have taken the listing if he had said they didn't need all that room anymore because he saw the error of his ways and planned to donate the stuffed animals to a wildlife museum. I considered listing it and posting it on PETA's website so they could educate him. Instead, I just nodded and tried to smile a lot, and got out of there as fast as I could. It's much easier for me to deal with people issues than animal issues.

People...Some days I come home and remove everything from my kitchen counters—I wouldn't want anything to suggest that I might have a hoarding issue. Although my collection of poodle figurines, plates, crocheted bottle covers, clocks, bobbleheads, and planters belies that. In my wildest imagination, I wouldn't have expected what I saw at the next most memorable home I sold.

Caller: "I'd like you to come over and talk to me about selling the house." That simple statement was no portent of what was to come.

The home was in a lovely, upscale neighborhood. As I walked up the uneven path to the door, past the dead lawn, I tried to give it the benefit of the doubt. Some people aren't into yard work. The window in the front door was covered with political stickers, so I had no warning of what lay behind it before the man opened the door. He was standing in a tunnel. A tunnel composed of stacked newspapers, boxes of all sizes, clothing—the light from the open door providing what little illumination of the inside there was.

"Doesn't look that bad from the outside, does it?" He grimaced.

As he led me through the tunnel to the family room where he had carved out a working space, he told me that his brother had died three months before, and it took him that long to burrow through to all the rooms.

"Why don't you just rent a dumpster and shovel it all out?" I asked.

"I can't. My brother has coin collections, pink slips to twelve collector cars, guns, you name it, it's in here."

Brother had a serious drinking problem, which was enabled by the trust fund that Dad set up for him. He would rotate the Jaguars and Ferraris from the backyard that wasn't large enough to hold them all to the street where the neighbors would report them, the police would tag them after three days, they'd be impounded, and he would bail them out. In fact, he died of cirrhosis of the liver while parked in one of the Jags at a gas station.

The living room was used to restore motorcycles, and battery acid had eaten through the slab floor. A linen closet held unopened boxes from Tiffany. I heard a beautiful chiming clock and commented on it.

"I'll sell it to you. My brother paid $800 for it; you can have it for $50." I don't think it's a good idea to buy personal property from clients, so I declined.

He thought I should buy the DeLorean car: "It would really jazz up your Realtor image," he said. Fortunately, it was a two-door.

So I stopped commenting on all the collectibles and we got down to business. It took him three more months to get the contents appraised, sold, and moved. Then we had to clean the house. I'd never been in a home where Merry Maids refused to work. They do everything. But refuse they did, on the grounds of it being a health hazard.

"What do I do now?" I asked their manager.

And that was my introduction to Crime Scene Cleaners, who specialize in suicide, homicide, and crime scene cleanup. I did not have them in my Rolodex. They did a miraculous job, and we got the home sold. But I still see that house in my dreams.

Another home I can't forget belonged to a couple who called me out in anticipation of refinancing, to determine the value of their home. "I haven't done a thing around the house in two weeks because my husband has been home with the flu," Mrs. said. Their tunnels were only waist-high. The kitchen counters were stacked half-way to the ceiling with dirty dishes, pots, and pans. The focal point of the property was the swimming pool—an in-ground plastic-liner pool, with a tree growing up from the center. A ten-foot tree. It had been longer than two weeks since anything had been done around the house.

They couldn't pull as much cash out of it as they wanted, so they listed it for sale with me. I thought, "Who would buy this?" But soon after planting the sign in the yard, a couple materialized for whom the home was perfect, they said. Forty-five days was long enough to close escrow, but a real push for the owners to empty the house.

A year later I dropped by, and nothing had changed but the owners and their clutter. New tunnels were carved through new piles of things that had dropped and been left where they fell. The pool tree was a foot higher. It must be a popular decorating style because, although I don't see it often, when I do the home sells quickly.

There's a buyer for every home.

Chapter 21

Love Me, Love My Dog, Cat, Iguana...

In real estate there are two categories of pets: pets that can get you into trouble (tenants' pets) and pets that can do no wrong (homeowners' pets).

I have a couple of landlords who learned the hard way that they don't want pets. One even said to me that when his wife's two Yorkshire terriers die, he'll "mourn for all of two minutes." He has to deal with their incontinent behinds and refuses to clean up after any others. He really hates cats—ever since his eccentric tenant collected twelve that sprayed everything within their reach, forcing him to replace drywall, subfloor, appliances, window coverings, and everything else inside the house.

That creates anxiety for me because: (A) I love dogs, and (B) it's against the law to discriminate against service pets. It's hard to comply with his wishes, especially when there are groups that hunt for Realtors who abuse these laws and prosecute the violators.

Whenever a potential tenant with a dog or cat calls and asks if we will consider a pet, I answer, "It depends." California and federal law define service animal as a dog that has been specifically trained to assist a person with his disability. Federal law also permits a trained miniature horse to be a service animal. They have little neck tags and official documentation. They've actually undergone training. But it gets complicated. A disabled person can self-proclaim his need for a service animal, and the only documentation required is written verification by a medical professional, or sometimes just a letter from the tenant explaining why he needs this animal for his disability. No training. No tag. No way out.

One day, I got a call from a nice young lady who wanted to see Mr. Kiljoy's rental. We met at the house, she walked through it, and then announced to me that "I have a service dog and you can't refuse to rent to me." Gulp. She was right. I called Mr. Kiljoy and told him he'd better pray that she didn't complete a lease application.

Things are so much more black and white with a sale. You either have the money or you don't. Doesn't matter what baggage you're bringing with you. But with rentals, we agents must use every bit of our gray matter to debate pet policy with inventive tenants:

"I have three Rottweilers. You don't take dogs? Mine go to work with me every day."

"My toy poodle never comes in the house."

"I train service dogs." That one necessitated a call to our attorney.

Dealing with homeowners' pets is much more straightforward: they can do no wrong. In San Francisco, dogs outnumber children. If you don't like animals, fake it because if the owner can't tell, the dog can. One of my clients subjects everyone who comes to her home to the "doggy test." I asked what that was.

"If my dog won't go up to him, he's not a good person," she stated with conviction.

Well, coming from a client, that's a valid test. For the record, let me say that I have never been rejected by a dog. It's a gift. I can remember the dogs' names better than the kids' names. Maybe it's because theirs hint at who they are: Dottie would be a Dalmatian, Bruiser would be a handful, and Georgie Girl would be, well, confused.

Everything that goes wrong concerning the homeowner's beloved pet is probably the agent's fault. I should not have told an appraiser, "Use my lockbox. There's a dog, but don't worry—he's really friendly and loves everyone." Apparently, male appraisers were the exception because the dog bit him.

I was to blame when Nixon, the seeing eye dog reject (potty issues), forgot two years' and $20,000 worth of training in a single afternoon.

Nixon's mom: "Cathy, we got home after your open house and found Nixon in the living room. He never goes in the living room."

Me: "Oh. I invited him to sit with me while visitors toured."

Nixon's mom: "And he won't eat his dog food. He usually has a voracious appetite."

Me: "Try a tuna fish sandwich."

Did Buster the Himalayan cat get in trouble when he expressed his opinion of all those agents and lookey-lous traipsing through his house? No! His owner never commented on the pile of personal waste he deposited smack dab in the middle of the champagne-colored living room carpet.

The greatest threat to my personal safety came from an African grey parrot. "Chatwyk" belonged to Dr. DoALot prior to his marriage. The bird hated the doctor's new wife to the extent that he would attack her whenever she sat on the sofa, which he had shared exclusively with the good doctor before Mrs. appeared on the scene.

Dr. D. thought Chatwyk would be happier if he had his own honey, so he bought him a lovely female Cockatoo. That's when the feathers hit the fan. Not only did the African grey try to defeather Cleo(patra), he went with even greater vengeance after everyone who entered their house. I lost a pair of earrings to him. But it all worked out in the end, because Dr. DoALot began to see Chatwyk's point of view, and the couple divorced shortly after I sold them their ~~nightmare~~ dream home.

Walk softly and carry a big bag of treats.

Chapter 22

Family, A Morality Play— Protect that ~~Gift~~ Down Payment to the Kids

Prescience is a perk we Realtors acquire after years of watching others make life-altering decisions—the omniscient perspective we get from our rearview mirrors. Don't you just know how some things will turn out? Like giving kids the down payment for a house. Why, sometimes I feel like Woody Allen directing a morality play.

One day while walking the farm I came upon a rather feeble-looking octogenarian trying to cut his lawn with a push mower.

"I'd sure love to move to a retirement place and give up all this yard work," he said.

"Well, I bet you can," I answered. "You're an original owner; your mortgage was probably paid off years ago. What's stopping you?" He laughed.

"I refi'ed to give each of the kids a down payment on their homes." The kids who couldn't help Dad with the yard work.

Why do otherwise intelligent and caring human beings, who make their children brush their teeth so they don't fall out, look both ways before crossing the street, and send them to college, lovingly set them up for failure by effectively saying, "Here, take the fruits of my labor which I (not you) toiled years to earn, with no (enforceable) strings attached, given willingly with the implicit message that the best things in life can be had for free. Go forth into the real estate market secure in the belief that someone will always rescue you"? Are we teaching them well?

Sylvia Browne, a renowned psychic, said, "You have to take care of Number One before you can help anyone else." A *psychic* said that. Is the gratification of giving the kids all that money worth the risk to your own security later in life? Don't play Russian roulette with the roof over your own head. Maybe it's a drop in your bucket, but think of the message you send. When you live within your means and don't overextend yourself, when you're that rock the family can come to in times of emergency (buying a house is not an emergency), you teach them to do the same. Show, don't tell.

Some parents know the right answer when asked to pluck feathers from their nest (egg). They just need a little reinforcement:

Smart Dad: "I don't know what to do. I mean, I loaned my daughter and her husband the down payment, he quit his job, and now they're in foreclosure and want me to bail them out."

Me: "OK. Let me see if I understand this correctly. You gave them $50,000, and they don't seem to be trying too hard to preserve and protect it."

"No, I *loaned* it to them."

As Len Tillem, the "People's Lawya" in Sonoma, California, tells his radio audience: "If you make a loan to a family member, consider it a gift." They did.

"Well, Smart Dad, I know you love your daughter dearly, but in your heart of hearts, how do you feel about her husband ~~abusing your trust and generosity~~?" I knew what he was thinking, so I just verbalized it for him. He needed a few booster calls afterward, but he did the right thing, the hard thing: He said no.

Like daylight saving time rolling around every year, I could count on an annual phone call from another dad whose daughter wanted to buy a house at least once a year. Dad was a self-made multimillionaire and could easily have bought her silence. But he wanted her to earn the satisfaction of owning a home the traditional way—by working for it. So every year he'd call me up and the three of us would drive over to this year's pick, and I would explain to her why it would not be a good investment. I won't admit to collusion because that's illegal, but Dad and I thought alike. Eventually she saved enough money to buy a condo.

Raising kids is a science project; the laws of nature prevail.

If you are a parent, you may be squirming in your seat right now, about to stop reading my book, thinking, "Cathy, you are cruel! You advocate child abuse. My child would never reneg on a promise." And you could be right; there are always exceptions to the rules...anomalies in nature. But here are some alternatives to save you and your offspring from possible financial and moral ruin.

First assumption: you are the parent, not a friend or other relation. Second: you have the financial means to help your kids buy a home. If not, well, think of it as a blessing in disguise that they have to work for it.

Speaking from my rearview mirror, I would not take a financial risk for anyone but direct, bloodline (or legally adopted) offspring—the ones who can guilt you out of sleep at night.

Scenario Number One: Friends with Benefits

Forget the usual innuendo; this is all about the parent-child relationship. Thinking of each other as friends (whom you can't push as far as you can parents) puts a little distance between you. The *benefits* are the money you inject:

- You lend the kids the down payment (mortgage companies typically want a letter saying this is a gift, not a loan, and will either require a gift letter signed by you, or the money seasoned in the kids' bank account for two months).

- They qualify for the loan on their own and purchase the home.

- After close of escrow, you go on title—perfectly legal.

The beauty of this approach is that the kids have to qualify for the loan—prove that they can afford to live there (thanks to your help). This minimizes your exposure; they can't refinance (further encumber) or even sell the house without your permission because you are on title. You can hover over your down payment.

The downsides:

- The kids could stop making payments to the bank (and/or you), and if they default, you're on title—it will appear on your credit report as well as on theirs. But you won't be liable for repayment of the loan.

- Litigiously speaking, if anything bad happens at the property, you could be pursued. And you don't have to be guilty to need a lawyer.

Scenario Number Two: Lease Option

The preferred choice. In simple terms, rent-to-buy. You, most benevolent parent, buy the house in your name, lease it to the kids, and let them buy it from you at a later date. Lease options have their downsides, too:

- The purchase price is agreed upon and must be honored months or years from the date, regardless of whether the market goes up or down. Good for the buyer, bad for the seller, but it's all in the family.

- The buyer pays option consideration, usually

several thousand dollars, which can be collected up front or monthly. If the option is not exercised, the buyer forfeits his down payment.

- Effectively, the lease option creates a landlord/tenant relationship with all the inherent issues that go with rental property.

I don't recommend lease options *except* in the parent to son or daughter situation. There are some things you do for love. It's an expedient that can work well for families.

Why do I prefer Scenario Number Two? Think of it as having the kids audition to own property. Over a period of time they'll prove they're worthy of your cash infusion by making timely rent payments. They'll establish a track record with a landlord (you), which lenders insist on. They'll prove they're responsible and serious by fixing whatever credit issue stopped them from qualifying before. Or not. But if they don't become models of tenant virtue, you've lost little or nothing. You can sell the house to someone else, and that person can become the kids' landlord.

If (Scenario Number One) the kids can qualify for a mortgage on their own but you're not convinced your down payment money is safe with them, insist on a lease option until which time you feel comfortable with less control over your money or until they give you a grandchild—you'll do anything they ask, then.

Here's how to do a lease option:

- Talk to a lender and determine what the kids would qualify for if they had a down payment or when they overcome the credit issue or whatever it is that's preventing them from buying. Don't fluff on this. You'll want them to be able to buy the home from you eventually. Lease optioning is just a stopgap measure.

- Add the loan amount to the down payment which is typically 20 percent for owner-occupied loans; that should be your target purchase price. Do not exceed that, no matter how much the kids beg. It's "get real" time.

- Hire a Realtor and let the kids choose their new home.

- Visit the real estate attorney and have him or her explain structuring and all the technicalities of lease options. If you decide to proceed, go back to the attorney to draw up the lease option documents. Realtors can do this, but I think it's better to have an attorney do it.

- Buy the home. Have the attorney prepare the

lease option concurrently so that everything is in place when you close escrow.

You may get some negative feedback from the kids on these suggestions. They whine, "Why can't we buy a bigger house?" "We want the tax write-off now," etc. Remind them that home ownership is not a right—it's the American Dream. Then silently say to yourself, *I've minimized my risk*. Because no matter how wonderful the kids are, nothing is without risk—especially real estate.

Save families! Advise parents to think of themselves as fiduciaries, not ATMs.

Chapter 23

Just Give Me Ten More Minutes—Timesavers

The most important thing you need to learn in real estate is time management. No matter how much time is allotted for a task, you always need more. I was quite effective at prioritizing until I started writing this book. So, if you're thinking about writing a book, you need to choose between earning a living and teaching others how to do it.

If you don't plan your day, others will do it for you, and they have far more pressing priorities than yours. As you scan the following time-saving tips you may say to yourself, "These are so obvious. This is not new information." And you'd be right. But, don't you ever get so caught up in the pressures of the day that you just react instead of thinking things through? That you forget your goal: to get through those twenty-four hours as effectively and efficiently as possible? *That you just lose it?!* Then these reminders will help:

1. Don't strive for perfection. Apostasy, you say! But how many of your "to-dos" just need to get done? No one will ever know that your new web page has only three of the five cute graphics you had considered posting. Or that the message you wrote to a client could be more eloquently stated. True, they are the products of your creative genius and it feels good to reflect on what a great job you did, but that takes time.

2. First thing in the morning, scan e-mail. Save the messages from Amazon and Coach Factory Online for later; usually those sales last at least twenty-four hours. Look for subject lines like Sorry, Buyer's Bailing; Your Lockbox Is Missing; and What Does Mold Look Like? Limit your e-mail consumption throughout the day.

3. Feared things first. Don't spend all your emotional energy dreading the task. Just jump on it and get it done.

4. Complete one task at a time, or get as far as you can on it for the day. Think FIFO (first in, first out). It forces you to deal with things that you may want to shove to the bottom of the pile.

5. If you're a morning person, like me, try to schedule appointments for the afternoon. Tackle the thought-intensive, brain-wracking tasks for your most productive hours. They take much less time when you have the energy. I don't have a creative thought after 2 p.m. or after lunch—whichever comes first. And, speaking of lunch, don't eat a big one; all that energizing oxygen will desert your brain and loll around in your tummy.

6. Schedule one day of the week for absolutely getting through (or at least going through) everything that you relegated to the "to do" basket. That way you won't worry about missing a deadline because you know you'll be pawing through the pile every Monday or Tuesday or whenever. You'll be a lot freer to put noncritical things to the side and deal with important stuff in a timely manner.

7. Set a timer. You'll find yourself moving more quickly through a task if you limit the time allotted. Knowing that an audible alarm will notify you also frees you from clock-watching.

8. Take a nap. Many companies in Japan work that into their employees' schedules. There's

something about stepping away from the desk, lying horizontally, sleeping, or just hovering in that between state that works magic on brain chemistry. You return refreshed and more creative. Again, set a timer. Naps can backfire.

9. Screen calls. You knew this already. We all do it. It's good for business. Who wants to be greeted by a frazzled agent, rushing through the call that interrupted her dispatching an ambulance for her client who was doing his own electrical repairs? You'll be so much nicer on the phone. If I do pick up a call mid-message, I ingratiate myself with the caller by saying "You're special; that's why I picked up."

10. Say "No." This one's hard because we Realtors are people-pleasers. But self-preservation demands that we not do everything we're asked nor accept every invitation we receive. There are lots of things that would be nice to do, but you're in business. And there's only one you.

11. Eliminate the file-shred time suck. Didn't you just hate it when they brought California Legal Code Sections 1798.80-1798-84 to our attention? I welcome mindless activity; it's refreshing. But mincing thousands of pages of

personal information into confetti every year? Well, I'd rather suck eggs.

You could solve this challenge by tossing those old files into the dumpster at your condo listing, as a broker (a broker!) I know did. Or you could follow my lead. This is another money-saving tip you get from buying my book which cost 3 percent of what Shred Happy wanted to charge me: I hired a tree-chipper who came to my house and made compost out of my old files.

12. Read the newspaper at night when it's too late to do anything about it. Why ruin the day by learning that *The Times* says it just turned from a seller's to a buyer's market? Your clients will tell you if there's anything you need to know before cocktail hour.

Finding enough hours in the real estate day is a challenge. But, busy multitasking Realtor that you are, you're up to it!

Remember:
Work expands to fill
the time allotted.

Conclusion

Do You Have What It Takes to Be a Realtor?

You may, at this point, want to call me and ask, "Cathy, could I make it if I'm not genetically predisposed to being a Realtor as you were?" Or, alternatively, "Can I get a refund on this book?"[18]

Frankly, I had an unfair advantage. MyMotherTheRealtor, by virtue of being the parent, always knew more than I did. I could count on her to correct anything I said related to real estate. My BrotherTheRealtor and MyOtherBrotherTheRealtor were born knowing *everything* about *everything*. They remain MyBrothers to this day with all the associated

---

18   Yes. Limited to first five callers.

ramifications. What I'm saying here is that the lack of a strong mentoring pool could work in your favor.

Seriously, heredity did play a part in my career ~~default~~ choice. But that's not to say that you can't succeed famously if your path is more circuitous. First, though:

Consider Other Employment Options

- Brain Surgeon. Although a career in real estate can pay better, background in this field equips you to determine if the client's behavior is physiological or psychological. Thus informed, you can stay on track when confronted with aberrant, non-buying behavior. Inquire if they took their meds today. Could couples therapy resolve the issue? Trips to and from property showings give you ample time to get to the bottom of things.

- Pharmacist. True, $100,000 a year is tempting. But transfer that training to real estate and you can prescribe over-the-counter medications to clients, identify their symptoms as psychosomatic or contagious, and be a full-service Realtor. Never lose sight of your purpose.

- Psychic. You may not have been born intuitive. But guaranteed, get into real estate and it will come naturally. Pretty soon you'll be able to say to your buyers, *I can read your mind.*

It's important to identify your skills and know your strengths. I can state as a matter of fact that the only previous jobs I've never seen on agents' employment applications are ballerina, parole officer, and lumberjack. So good news—if you have no related experience it won't be a hindrance. There is no clear path to becoming a Realtor so no one can say you're unqualified, that you haven't done the time. And if, by unfortunate chance, you have done time and can explain away the felony, you're in.

Consider the Health Risks

Be warned: real estate is a blood condition. Symptoms include a constant ringing in the ears, identified by the American Medical Association as The Calling. It sounds a lot like the *uhoooga!* tone you set on your cell phone to identify incoming client calls.

It's extremely contagious (they say three-quarters of Americans experience a form of it to some degree), and can be transmitted over the phone, computer, and carrier pigeon when whacking the heck out of your smart phone does not produce the desired results. It can lie dormant for years between bull markets. There is no cure.

Get to Know the Players

Before you commit, socialize with professionals in related fields:

A. Appraisers. This, for example, would be a joke you could tell an appraiser at a party, if they went to parties: How do you determine the market value of a single-family dwelling? Answer: It's the square root of the parcel number. He wouldn't laugh, though, because appraisers are deadly serious. I know because I used to be one until I laughed convulsively at the annual cost to maintain my state appraiser's certification ($495 for continuing education and the license) versus $87 a year to maintain my real estate broker's license.

Conventions are a good place to get to know appraisers. If a real estate convention and an appraisal convention were held at the same time on the same floor at the same hotel, the appraisal convention would be mistaken for a wake. But they're really very nice people.

B. Home Inspectors. Learn the words that endear you to them: lead, asbestos, nonconforming use. When you invite one for coffee, mention mold—he'll pick up the check. Since you're not paying, invite a termite inspector. It will feel like yoga class, such perfect harmony; they both love finding things that are Wrong.

But someday, you'll tire of their dark writing style. Why can't they just be *mellow*, focus on the positive and let what's wrong be conspicuous by its absence? Well, that decides it. You'll make the happier choice—you'll be a Realtor!

C. Realtors. We can be found *everywhere*. For example, the following people I know have their real estate licenses:

- My hairdresser

- The owner of the corner Chinese restaurant

- My dentist's receptionist

- Half of my Facebook friends

Tour day at your local real estate board is a good place to get to know us. We are a very friendly group and bond well, especially to sellers. Identify yourself as a prospective Realtor versus a lender, home inspector, or home warranty rep, and car doors will open to you. Why? Because we feed on new agents. But don't let that scare you. Remember, you are there to learn. Choose your ride carefully. Realtors are great communicators. You'll learn more in our cars. And we'll even let you drive!

We Realtors congregate and can often be found at conventions and seminars, learning things. It costs money to attend them. Here's an important takeaway, insider information that you will only read here: Agents will give you the designer shirt off their back, their last cookie on tour day, but their secrets...you have to buy those. And they cost way more than this book that only set you back a venti four-shot caramel macchiatto, which makes learning *my* secrets a real bargain!

If you don't want to pay to get to know Realtors in their natural habitat, other places we can be found are the grocery store, the Department of Employment, and jury duty. I personally love jury duty and take advantage of every opportunity to get reimbursed for mileage.

Once You Have Committed, Set Goals

Worthy goals to have:

- Staying solvent. Adopt a reasonable budget. The profligate Realtor indulges in frequent business lunches with clients; the frugal Realtor researches Tuesday broker open house lists to determine who's serving the best food and feeds her family a good meal once a week.

- Study the teachings of wise life coaches such as Tony Robbins, Mahatma Gandhi, and Dave Barry.

- Have a backup plan that could include, for instance, a cosigner for a loan, a relative with extra bedrooms, and a kennel.

Ask yourself: *Can I afford to be in real estate?* I strongly recommend marriage or a codependent relationship.

Summary

True or False: As of January, 2013, one in two adults in the U.S. over the age of 18 was a real estate agent.[19] The median gross income for a real estate agent in 2012 was $43,500.[20] You could be one of those persons!

All that aside, why be a Realtor? It's not just about the money or that you can take naps whenever you want. It's the gratitude you see on your client's face when she says, "Thank God that's over!" It's knowing that humoring the players through the process not only helped them achieve their goal, but actually made it enjoyable. It's the security that we can never be replaced by a service center in a third world country, or by some

---

19 False. It was 1.2 licensed real estate agents per 100 normal people.
20 True.

app or a machine. (Although 3-D printers are getting frighteningly close.) When a Realtor shows up at a house, you know it's a live person!

Yes, there are days when I gaze out the window, watching the gardener blow leaves, thinking, "I could do that." When I walk past the accordionist at the train station with his dog on his back, tail wagging like a metronome in beat to the music, passersby tossing dollars at him, and imagine myself singing Broadway hits on a corner with my poodle holding a collection plate in his mouth. But the little voice in my head reminds me that no other career could be as rewarding.

Real estate sales *is* the American Dream. The opportunity, no matter what you Used To Be, to work like the devil for yourself and elevate your standard of living, to meet interesting people, to have a grasp of how the world works. It's the joy of successfully negotiating a person through one of life's most challenging transitions and being able to support your family doing it.

So, real estate agents and WannaBes, laugh your way to success. UsedToBes, reconsider? And, ThoseWhoLoveUs—we couldn't live without you.

Special Offers for Readers of this Book

Keep laughing, learning, and selling!

- **Cathy coaches**. Let's solve your real estate sales challenges together. Laugh the kinks out in my free monthly conference calls.

- Fire up your week with Monday/Wednesday/Friday **Motivational Messages** about real estate sales and marketing to keep you on track and laughing!

- Receive a sample of Cathy's **farming newsletter** with instructions on what to include, why to include it, where to find the information, and how to distribute it.

**Get these special offers at
www.CathyTurneyWrites.com/BookBonus**

Credits and Thanks

It took a village to get this book into print. Self-publishing looks easy until you try doing it all by yourself. My village consists of:

Howard VanEs of Let's Write Books, Inc., who brought me through the hybrid/indie publishing process with unflagging patience and brilliant advice. Check Howard out at www.LetsWriteBooks.net. Bless you, my friend.

Lisa Tener, book coach extraordinaire. Lisa got into my head and helped me spin these stories into teaching moments to help and inspire others. Lisa reads minds and can be found conducting her award-winning "Bring Your Book to Life" program at www.LisaTener.com.

Cynthia Rubin and Ruth Dunmire, my editors, who found countless exceptions to my rule of thumb that if I don't remember where the comma goes, probably no one else does, either. They spare me from public humiliation. Check *your* grammar and punctuation at www.MyGrammarGuru.com.

MyHusbandTheEngineer—Where do I begin? I march into the maw of technology, fearless, because John fixes everything that I break. And smiles while he's doing it. There is no greater love.

My surrogate sister, Monica, who bravely married into our family of Realtors and inspires and encourages me in writing and in life; and to her husband, MyBrotherTheRealtor, who rises to every occasion, personally and professionally. You both rock!

Bill Jansen and Leslie Walsh, legal team supreme. You keep hundreds of Realtors out of trouble every year with grace and humor and remain the best part of Better Homes.

To all of you friends who read my stories and laugh—you are the wind in my sails. And, my family of clients, I could get very mushy here so just know that the best part of my career has been helping you achieve your goals and becoming friends. I love you.

About the Author

With over 25 years' experience in real estate sales, Cathy Turney produces in the top 10 percent of all real estate agents nationally and is the real estate expert on Emmy Award–winning Judd McIlvain's Troubleshooter program. A real estate broker, Cathy is the managing partner at Better Homes Realty in Walnut Creek, California, where she has worked since 1993. Previously, she was an associate broker at Coldwell Banker Real Estate and RE/MAX. She was also one of the first residential appraisers to be licensed in California.

A native of Chicago, Cathy grew up in the San Francisco Bay Area and graduated from the University of California at Santa Cruz. She is a columnist for *The Concordian* newspaper and has been published in the *San Francisco Chronicle*, national magazines, and numerous websites. Her humor stories have won national awards, and her first book, *Dog Stories, Hilarious Tales of a Codependent Pet Owner*, was a best seller in its category on Amazon.

Cathy and her husband, John, live in Concord, California. In their spare time, they enjoy hanging out at the ocean with their rescue dogs in their RV, reading and wine tasting. When she's not trying to be the best real estate broker her clients could hire, Cathy volunteers and helps raise funds for animal welfare. Fifty percent of this book's proceeds will be donated to the Alameda Food Bank, Farm Sanctuary, and NorCal Poodle Rescue.

Stay in touch with Cathy at Cathy@cathyturney.com, her website, www.CathyTurneyWrites.com, on Google Plus at +Cathy Turney, and on Facebook at Cathy Turney.

Did You Enjoy This Book?

If you have enjoyed reading this book, please help others find it by posting a review on Amazon. If there is something you would like to see added or changed, please send a note to Publisher@RealEstateSuccessPress.com. Thank you and good selling!

Made in the USA
Charleston, SC
06 March 2015